Faith

Explaining Your
Faith
Without Losing Your Friends

ALISTER E.
McGRATH

Academie Books Grand Rapids, Michigan
Zondervan Publishing House

EXPLAINING YOUR FAITH
Copyright © 1988, 1989 by Alister E. McGrath

First Published in Britain by Inter-Varsity Press

First Zondervan edition 1989

ACADEMIE BOOKS is an imprint of Zondervan Publishing House
1415 Lake Drive, S.E., Grand Rapids, Michigan 49506

Library of Congress Cataloging in Publication Data

McGrath, Alister E., 1953-
  Explaining your faith / Alister E. McGrath.
    p.   cm.
  Bibliography: p.
  ISBN 0-310-29741-9
  1. Apologetics–20th century.   2. College students–Religious
life.   I. Title.
  BT1102.M35   1989
  239–dc19   89-5619
                                                             CIP

Designed by Jan M. Ortiz

Printed in the United States of America

90 91 92 93 94 / CH / 10 9 8 7 6 5 4 3 2

Contents

About this Book

"Always be prepared to give an answer to everyone who asks you to give the reason for the hope that you have" (1 Peter 3:15).

This is a book for students. It isn't an evangelism manual. It isn't a theological textbook. It is just meant to help you deal with some of the difficulties which people—especially students!—genuinely feel when they are considering the claims of Christianity. Obviously there isn't space enough to deal with all the difficulties people have with the gospel, just as there isn't space enough to give very detailed replies to these. So what you will find is a list of what seem to be the most common problems and objections, with outlines of what you might say in response to them, and recommended reading to allow you to follow up any points in further detail.

The college campuses of the world are the arenas in which a battle is being fought for the hearts and minds of men and women. It is hoped that this little book may be a useful resource in this struggle, in which the claims of Jesus Christ are presented, explained and defended in the face of a disbelieving world, which greatly wished it *could* believe.

Alister McGrath

Chapter 1

Introduction

Trying to explain Christianity to a non-Christian is rather like trying to explain falling in love to someone who's never had that experience. You could try and explain it in rather academic terms—like what it is that Christians believe. But this doesn't really convey the excitement of Christian faith, any more than a definition of "falling in love" can express what that really feels like!

Your non-Christian friends may try to invalidate your experience and behaviour—"He's got religion," or "She's fallen in with the Jesus crowd." They feel threatened by it—it's not something they can really understand. And so they try to dismiss it. But don't let this discourage you. Remember the famous words of the great German writer Goethe: "We are used to the fact that people make fun of things which they don't understand." Ridiculing your experience doesn't *invalidate* it—any more than ridiculing someone in love would invalidate the fact that he or she has fallen in love.

Two basic points you need to remember. First, to be of real help to your friends as they wrestle with Christianity, you must try and think yourself into their situation. You must empathize with them, to use the jargon. But, second, you can only truly empathize when you are honest with yourself and with your non-Christian friends about your faith and about the questions you yourself may have at times. This honesty does not invalidate your faith—and it certainly will not "turn off" your friends. Rather, it underscores the reality of the statement that evangelism is like one beggar telling another where to find bread. And it acknowledges that your faith does not rest on your own immutable understanding of God, but rather is trust in the God who is immutable in spite of our own lack of understanding and even (at times) of faith.

What is Christianity and how can we communicate it?

1. *Most people have very confused understandings of what Christianity is about!*

Most people don't reject Christianity because they have given it careful consideration and decided that it is wrong. In most cases, they encounter a caricature of Christianity, and reject that instead. For example, in the first century many civilized Romans rejected Christianity because they thought it involved cannibalism (can you see why?)—and it was necessary to explain to them what Christians were really doing when they met for worship. Don't worry if your friends seem to have the most unlikely ideas about what Christianity is like!

Slowly, you can begin to remove these obstacles to faith by explaining what Christianity is really like.

But before you can explain what Christianity is like, you need to have given the matter some thought yourself! Many Christians pay surprisingly little attention to the content of their faith. They concentrate upon experiencing God through prayer, Bible-reading and worship. Now this is no bad thing! But it does mean that you neglect an aspect of being a Christian that is important in evangelism of any sort—being able to explain what Christians believe, and why. (There are a number of books readily available which explain clearly and simply what Christians believe—and why—noted at the end of this chapter. Try to read some of them!)

When you try to explain Christianity, you may discover that some people feel very threatened by it. They may find it convenient to seize upon certain points as obstacles to faith. In other words, they use some argument against Christianity as an excuse for not thinking further about the claims of Jesus Christ. "Christianity is for the intellectually feeble." "I can't believe in God with all this suffering in the world." "Christianity is just for those who need a sense of purpose and meaning—and I don't." "Everybody knows that God is just an astronaut." Sometimes, of course, these are genuine difficulties, and must be treated with respect. There are answers to these objections.

Very often, however, these reasons are not genuine difficulties at all—they are simply ploys to prevent the discussion of Christianity from getting too intense or involved for comfort. Many non-Christians find any discussion of Christianity very threatening. They feel

9

that they are being attacked, and they dig in to their positions. Just as a drowning man might clutch at a straw, so they reach for the nearest defence against Christianity they can find. Occasionally, these objections to Christianity have been picked up second hand from books or magazine articles.

Why do many non-Christians find Christianity so threatening? Because Christianity involves a demand. It involves a demand for conversion, for a change of life. It involves repentance—an admission that you are wrong, that you are sinful. And these are difficult things for many people to accept. When you talk to your non-Christian friends about your faith, your friends may feel that you are passing judgment on them, and become very uncomfortable. Their natural response may well be to mount a counterattack by raising an objection to Christian belief—not necessarily because this is a genuine difficulty for them, but because it sidetracks the conversation in a less threatening direction (e.g., into a general discussion about the problem of suffering). Now it may be that your friend has genuine difficulties with this problem. Nevertheless, the main function of this tactic is generally to remove the personal threat felt from the way the discussion was going! The discussion can now be about how some philosophers handle a certain question—it is no longer about your friend and God!

Therefore, when you're discussing Christianity with your friends, you must realize that the claims of Jesus Christ are one element—by far the most important element, to be sure—in your discussion. The other element is the person you're talking to. And it is that second element which is all too easy to neglect. You are not arguing with a computer, or some sort of machine, but with fellow human beings. They will have emotions, feelings, and possibly deeply held views. You must be sensitive to their interests and feelings and avoid making it unnecessarily difficult for them to come to faith. Remember that your friends may well identify *you* with the Christian faith—and that means that you may put obstacles in their path to faith because of the way you relate to them. To become a Christian is a difficult enough decision—don't make it even more difficult for them because of the way you handle them. Try to make it as easy as possible for them to turn to Jesus Christ and his gospel.

A failure to deal sensitively with someone can be disastrous. You need to be aware of certain basic human emotions and feelings—like the need to feel that you have been listened to. Try to be a good listener. It may be that your friends have had experiences which have made it genuinely difficult for them to take Christianity seriously. It may be that they have a genuine difficulty which you can help resolve. Let them know that you are listening to them, and trying to understand them. Understanding people doesn't mean that you have to agree with them! If it is obvious that you are taking trouble to listen to them, they will find it much easier to listen to you.

Try to imagine what happens when one party to a discussion feels threatened by the way things are going, and so "digs in" to his position in such a way that he can't move without losing face. He will dig himself in by erecting defensive barricades that you can't penetrate. No amount of arguing will get you anywhere here. He doesn't want to give the impression of backing down. He may well feel that you are right—but he feels he will seem to lose face with you or with his circle of friends if he admits this. So how do you avoid this situation?

Suppose you're talking about an issue—let's say, the resurrection. Your friend spends some time explaining why he or she can't accept the idea. You could respond like this. "I can understand what you're saying. From your point of view, the resurrection must look rather improbable. I can sympathize with the way you feel. Let me explain how it looks from my point of view. Actually, I would see it in rather a different light...." Here you are being positive towards your friend, and making it easier for him or her to listen to your side of the dispute. A "lock-in" situation results when you fail to separate the people and the issue.

People tend to see their ideas as part of their person. This means that if you attack their ideas, you appear to be attacking them as persons. An attack on your friend's *view on the resurrection* may thus be seen as an attack on your *friend himself*, even though this isn't what you were intending. You must therefore be careful to distinguish between the two. Let's look at two different ways of handling your friend's difficulties with the resurrection. Let's suppose he's just finished listing his difficulties with the idea. Here are two responses, representing these different approaches.

> A: Well, I'm sorry, but you're wrong. These objections just aren't important. I can't take them seriously, and I don't think you've even bothered to think about them. I'm sure that if you were to think about them longer, you'd see that. Let's go

through these so-called objections that you've just made, and I'll show you how unimportant they really are.

B: I can understand just how you must feel about this. In fact, I once felt much the same way myself, and can really sympathize with you. Actually, I've changed my mind since then, and see it in a different way now. Let me try and explain the way I see it.

(A) tends to identify the person and his views, and suggests that you're trying to score points off him by beating him in argument. It's you and your ideas against him and his ideas. (B) makes it easy for your friends to make a distinction between themselves as persons and their ideas on the resurrection. You are avoiding attacking your friends unnecessarily. It suggests that you are trying to help them think the matter through (which is what you are, or ought, to be doing). You are seen as giving another perspective on the question, rather than as contradicting your friends. In short, you are making it much easier for your friends to listen to you. It isn't you against them as opponents, but you and them together trying to resolve something in which you're mutually interested. Nobody is going to lose face in this discussion. Your friendship will survive (B), and probably benefit from it—but (A) may well wreck it!

But sometimes it is not the other person who digs in and becomes defensive—it is we ourselves. The main reason for this is that we subconsciously feel that the other's arguments have some force, but we don't dare to face up to our own doubts. And as a result we start focusing on the truth of statements about God and Christ, rather than on God himself.

Removing obstacles to faith

You cannot argue people into the kingdom of God! It may be that you are able to win an argument with your non-Christian friends. For example, you may end up convincing them that God does indeed exist. But that still leaves them a long way from faith. In the end Christian faith comes about by meeting the risen Christ, not just by becoming convinced of the truth of some arguments! Christianity isn't just a list of propositions which you can tick off as you accept them. It is a matter of the heart, as well as the mind. And there's always the danger that you may win the argument, but lose your friend. Why bother, then, dealing with difficulties which people might have about Christianity? Because these difficulties are obstacles between them and God, which we are in a position to remove or at least to weaken. Your arguments won't bring them to faith—but they may remove obstacles in the path of that faith.

In *First and Second Things,* C. S. Lewis spoke of the value of "creating an intellectual (and imaginative) climate favourable to Christianity . . . If the intellectual climate is such that, when a man comes to a crisis at which he must either accept or reject Christ, his reason and imagination are not on the wrong side, then his conflict will be fought out under favourable conditions." Think of yourself as helping to create this "intellectual climate favourable to Christianity."

In the final analysis, of course, there is only one agent in evangelism, and that is God himself. It is his gospel and his power; wisdom and strength lie behind it. Our

14

task as believers is to point people in the right direction, so that they may encounter the living God. In John's gospel we find a very helpful pointer to the nature of evangelism (John 1:43–51). Philip tells Nathanael that he has found the person about whom Moses and all the prophets wrote—Jesus of Nazareth. Nathanael immediately raises objections to this. How can such a person come from Nazareth, of all places?

Philip might have begun a long argument about how this objection wasn't as serious as might at first seem. He might have appealed to the same prophecy that we find cited in Matthew's gospel (Matthew 2:23). But rather than get involved in a rather contentious argument about Old Testament prophecy and the merits of Nazareth as a town, Philip issues a simple and direct invitation: "Come and see!" (John 1:46). And, as the remainder of the passage makes clear, it is Jesus who captures Nathanael's heart and mind (John 1:47-51).

Or again, think of John the Baptist (Mark 1:1–9); John 1:15–36). He pointed people away from himself, to the one who was greater than himself. He was like a herald, a royal forerunner, proclaiming the coming of the king. Like him, we point away from ourselves, away from our own faith—and we point to Jesus Christ, the one who is greater than we, upon whom our faith is based.

It is our job to be a signpost—like Philip and John the Baptist. We too have to point people away from ourselves and towards the living Christ. It isn't our arguments which will bring someone to faith—it is a personal encounter with the risen Christ. We may help create conditions favourable to that encounter. Our task is to remove impediments to this encounter. What sort of impediments?

Misunderstandings of what Christianity is all about, for a start. Genuine intellectual obstacles, such as doubts about the fundamental goodness or love of God. Ignorance about what to do in order to become a Christian. A reluctance to admit to being a sinner. All these, and many others, are obstacles placed between individuals and the God who loved them so much that he gave his only Son to die for them (John 3:16).

This is not to say that we can remove all the obstacles to faith for our friends! For, in the end, the greatest obstacles which come between an individual and God is that individual's sin. Only that individual can deal with this sin, by recognizing and admitting it and receiving forgiveness from God. What we can do is to show our friends that it is sin which is the real obstacle between them and the living God. By removing, or helping to reduce, other difficulties in the path of faith, we can explain what the real difficulty is, and how it may be resolved. This is the task of evangelism—to identify the real problem (human sin), and proclaim (and explain!) the one genuine solution (divine forgiveness).

"I'm no good at evangelism"

At this point, however, you may find yourself thinking, "Evangelism isn't for me. I'd be no good at it" (If that's not what you're thinking, read on anyway!). Actually, this is the best place to start. It's good to recognize your personal inadequacy—but you need to move on, and see that this isn't quite as important as you think.

You need to recognize both your personal inadequacy, and the irrelevance of this inadequacy to evangelism. It is natural to think that the really effective communicators of the gospel are high-powered, competent and confident. But how many of us are like that? Most of us have enough insight to realize how inadequate we are!

However, the New Testament makes it abundantly clear that God's power works through human weakness (e.g., see 1 Corinthians 2:3–5; 2 Corinthians 4:7, 12:7–10). The cross of Jesus Christ—something which the world then thought was (and still thinks is) weak and foolish—is a symbol of the Christian realization that God works through weakness. It isn't what we are that matters—it's what we let God do with us that really counts. Two important points may be made here.

First, acknowledging our own weakness and inadequacy is actually the first step in turning to God, to ask him for power, strength and wisdom. By recognizing how weak we are, we find it easier to turn to God and claim his strength. After all, it is God's gospel, given and entrusted to us—and we need to learn to rely upon him as we proclaim his gospel in his world. Self-confidence and self-reliance are seriously out of place in the Christian life: the only real ground of confidence is God (1 Corinthians 1:31; 3:21). Prayer is thus an acknowledgment both of our own inadequacy and God's ability to meet our needs.

Second, acknowledging our weakness reminds us of something it is very easy to overlook—that Christianity is not based upon human wisdom, but upon the power of God (see 1 Corinthians 2:3–5). Christianity doesn't make its appeal to some sort of intellectual elite. It isn't based upon contemporary academic wisdom, which is outdated in decades rather than centuries. Anyone who has studied the history of ideas is aware of just how

17

quickly ideas go out of fashion. They are abandoned, rather than refuted. Underlying the gospel is something which cannot go out of date—the power of God.

The gospel proclaims that the human problem is basically the same today as it always has been—selfish human nature, existing in a sinful fallen world. And the gospel does not merely diagnose this situation, but offers a remedy. So long as men and women seek after truth, the gospel proclamation that Jesus Christ is "the way, the truth and the life" (John 14:6) will remain a challenge to human wisdom. So long as human beings walk the face of this earth, knowing that they must die, the gospel proclamation of eternal life will continue to be relevant.

We have not been entrusted with some sort of intellectual or spiritual consumer product with a shelf-life of a few centuries, but with the transforming and creative power of God at work in his world. The gospel will not and cannot go out of date! The gospel is about the living God, who comes to us in Jesus Christ and makes himself available for us. It is especially important for students to grasp this point: they will not be committing themselves to some system of belief which will go out of date within a decade. The gospel has stood the twin tests of time and experience for two thousand years, without giving any indication of being "irrelevant" or "outdated" yet!

So if you feel inadequate—don't worry! All of us are inadequate. And by recognizing your inadequacy, you will be all the more likely to trust in God, and not yourself. By recognizing our weakness and lack of wisdom, we turn to God, in order to receive his strength and wisdom. God uses us—but, in the end, he doesn't

18

depend upon us. The graveyards of the world are packed full of people who thought that Christianity depended upon them—but the grave couldn't hold the one upon whom Christianity really depends: the risen Christ. And it is by claiming his power and presence, and by pointing people to him, that we best serve him.

In this introductory chapter, we've been looking at some points worth noting as you try to explain Christianity to your friends. They may help you avoid some obvious mistakes. But, as we noted right at the beginning, there is no substitute for thinking through the main points of the Christian faith yourself. You can get away with "Actually, I don't know!" or "I haven't thought about that one!" every now and then—but when it becomes a regular occurrence, you aren't likely to be terribly helpful to anyone interested in learning more about Christianity. The remainder of this little book is an attempt to help you think about the main points of the Christian faith, so that you can explain it and defend it to your interested friends. We begin by going right to the core of the Christian faith, as we begin to think about Jesus Christ himself.

Questions for discussion
- What are the key points of the Christian faith?
- Why should evangelism be people-centred?
- Is the messenger as well as the message important in evangelism?
- What personal qualities are helpful in evangelism?

For further reading
C. S. Lewis, **Mere Christianity.** This is probably one of the best, and certainly one of the most famous and readable,

introductions to Christianity. The reputation of C. S. Lewis seems to be growing all the time, and this work is ideal to give to a friend to start them thinking. It is always available in print—and if your friend likes it, there are plenty of other works by C. S. Lewis to try next. His autobiography **Surprised by Joy** would be an excellent next step, as in this book Lewis describes his own journey to faith, listing and meeting many of the difficulties he had on the way. Many students, especially those studying literature, will find this a fascinating work.

There are a number of other books which you might also find helpful:

David Cook, **Thinking about Faith.** A useful introduction to the key points of the Christian faith.

Michael Green, **World on the Run.** A splendid challenge to those who think that Christians are running away from reality.

Michael Green, **You must be Joking!** An examination of a wide range of objections made to Christian belief, with very helpful responses.

Francis Schaeffer, **The God Who is There.** A very powerful affirmation of the reality of God.

John Stott, **Basic Christianity.** A classic presentation of Christianity, tried and tested over many years.

Chapter 2

Jesus

Since the coming of Jesus, history has never been the same. Two great epochs—before Christ and after Christ—are defined. It's one of the little ironies of history that we date everyone and everything (including those who did their best to exterminate Christianity!) with reference to this one man. For the Roman historian Livy, everything was to be dated with reference to the founding of Rome. But for western culture, everything is to be dated with reference to the birth of Jesus Christ. Even the lives of those who were utterly opposed to Jesus Christ and all that he stood for are dated with reference to him! Thus the Roman emperor Nero died in A.D. 68, and the great dictator Joseph Stalin in A.D. 1953.

But what relevance does Jesus have for us? Why is it that Christianity centres upon this man? Even at this stage, a number of very serious misunderstandings arise as non-Christians attempt to make sense of Jesus' relevance for the Christian. For example, a Marxist might assume that Jesus has the same relevance for Christianity that Karl Marx has for Marxism. He's the person who introduced some new ideas into history. Of course, a Marxist might say, Jesus' ideas had to be modified (didn't they?), in much the same way as Marx's ideas had to be modified by Engels, Lenin or Mao Tse Tung. And even some less-informed Christians seem to think that this is why Jesus is so important for Christianity. In this chapter, we're going to look at a number of important misunderstandings and objections which you are likely to come across as you try to explain Christianity to your friends.

One important point needs to be made before we do this. Some Christians tend to assume that people are either totally for Christ, or totally opposed to him. In fact, the situation is much more complex. Many people feel sympathetic to Jesus, yet wouldn't regard themselves as Christians. They may, for example, be prepared to accept Jesus as a great teacher, or perhaps as a prophet—but not to accept him as Saviour and Lord. Now this step may take place very suddenly—but it may also take place in a number of stages. For example, someone might begin by believing that Jesus didn't really exist. Then they might abandon this position, and start to think of Jesus as a good religious teacher. And finally, they might come to believe in him as Lord and Saviour.

So be sensitive: try to work out how far your friends are in their thinking, and see if you can help them further along. And don't get discouraged if you find you only make slow progress—you may be helping your friend take a further step along the road which leads to faith. Now it may well be the case that you can help them come fully to faith. But don't necessarily become anxious if you are unable to help them believe in Jesus as Lord and Saviour straight away! Perhaps your friend may begin by believing that Jesus didn't actually exist, and end up thinking of Jesus as a prophet. Later you, or perhaps someone else, can help them take the final steps. The important thing is to leave someone further along the road to faith in Christ than they were to begin with.

Objection: Jesus didn't exist anyway

This is an objection which isn't taken terribly seriously by anyone, but which you may still come across occasionally. The New Testament witness to Jesus is just too consistent and coherent to make this suggestion plausible. To account for it in other ways involves bringing in a whole series of rather improbable hypotheses. In the end, the simplest, neatest and most plausible explanation of the evidence is that Jesus of Nazareth existed as a historical person.

Perhaps, however, someone might point out that Paul hardly ever makes reference to the earthly life of Jesus. This is true, in one respect—Paul is intensely interested in Jesus' death on the cross and his resurrection, but seems to make little reference to the details of Jesus' earthly life. But why should he anyway? Paul encountered the risen Christ—as have so many since him—and insists that it is this risen Christ, rather than the historical figure of Jesus of Nazareth, which is central to Christianity. We can hardly draw the conclusion that Jesus didn't exist on the basis of this evidence!

A further point concerns the nature of Paul's writings. The writings of Paul preserved in the New Testament are *letters*. They aren't history textbooks! It isn't relevant to Paul's purpose to go over the details of Jesus' life—he assumes that his readers already know these. But even here, Paul often recalls the teaching of Jesus. This is especially clear in 1 Corinthians, in which Paul frequently calls upon the authority of Jesus to make a point (1 Corinthians 7:10; 9:14; 11:23–25). Paul argues that his teaching here goes back to the words of Jesus himself.

Paul's teaching at other points also seems to go back to the words of Jesus. It is clear that his emphasis falls upon the relevance of the risen Christ to the Christian church, but that he draws upon the teaching authority of the earthly Jesus at points. Once more, there is no reason whatsoever to draw the extravagant conclusion that Jesus didn't exist. It's like the suggestion that it was really Judas who died on the cross, or that Jesus wandered off to India after the disciples thought he had died: they are all suggestions which are totally unwarranted by the historical evidence.

Objection: You can't trust the New Testament documents

But, it might be argued, the New Testament is biased. After all, it was written by Christians. We need independent confirmation of what the New Testament says about Jesus. We need to look at other sources. But what sources are there? Our main sources for a knowledge of any aspect of the first century are Roman historians. These historians are few in number in the first place, and their writings largely exist as fragments. And they could hardly have foreseen that what seemed in the first century to be nothing more than an obscure Palestinian sect would one day come to dominate the Roman Empire! Judea was a backwater of the Roman empire, to which nobody paid much attention in the first place. And anyway, thousands of Jewish agitators were crucified in Judea under the Romans: one more would have passed unnoticed. In fact, we find exactly what we might expect: Roman historians pay no attention to Christianity at all, except when it caused social or political disturbances. Even then, their chief interest concerns these disturbances, rather than the basis of the beliefs of those who were causing them.

In the modern period, of course, news gathering has become much more sophisticated. News analysts can be jetted to any part of the world immediately to report on events which seem important. Their back-up teams can then provide in-depth analysis. But in the first century, Roman historians were based at Rome, and had to use material readily available to them. There was just no way that they could have known that seemingly unimportant events in an obscure provincial backwater would one day shake the empire to its foundations!

Having said that, we do find reference to Jesus in four classical authors of the first or early second centuries. These are Thallus (a first century Greek writer with a particular interest in relating Roman history to the history of the eastern Mediterranean, referred to by Julius Africanus in the third century); Pliny the Younger, writing c. A.D. 111 to Trajan about the rapid spread of Christianity in Asia Minor: Tacitus, who wrote c. A.D. 115 concerning the events of A.D. 64, in which Nero made Christians the scapegoats for the burning of Rome; and Suetonius, writing c. A.D. 120 concerning certain events in the reign of the emperor Claudius.

Suetonius refers to a certain "Chrestus" who was behind rioting at Rome. "Chrestus" was still an unfamiliar name to Romans at this stage, whereas "Christus" was a common name for slaves (meaning "someone who is useful"). Even in the third and fourth centuries, Christian writers were still complaining about people who misspelled "Christus" as "Chrestus"!

What do these pagan authors tell us about Jesus? Not as much as we would like! Nevertheless, we can draw the following conclusions from their writings.

1. Christ had been condemned to death by Pontius Pilate, procurator of Judea, during the reign of the Roman emperor Tiberius (Tacitus). Pilate was procurator of Judea from A.D. 26–36, while Tiberius reigned from A.D. 14–37. The traditional date for the crucifixion is A.D. 30–33.

2. At the time of the crucifixion, there seems to have been some sort of supernatural darkness, which some explained in terms of a total eclipse of the sun (Thallus).

3. By the time of Nero, Christ had attracted sufficient followers in Rome to make them a suitable scapegoat for the burning of Rome. These followers were named "Christians" after him (Tacitus).

4. "Chrestus" was the founder of a distinctive sect within Judaism (Suetonius).

5. In A.D. 111, Christians worshipped Jesus as if he were God, abandoning the worship of the Roman emperor to do so (Pliny).

These historical details tie in well with the New Testament accounts. Fragmentary though they are, they are remarkably consistent with the New Testament witness.

But what about the allegation that the New Testament

is biased? In one sense, it is obvious that this point is valid. The New Testament writers are out to win faith. They believe that their accounts of Jesus' life, death and resurrection ought to evoke faith in their readers (John 20:31–32). But in another sense, the point is not valid: the assumption of many critics of Christianity seems to be that the New Testament is inaccurate, perhaps deliberately distorting history for its own ends. New Testament scholarship has, however, actually tended to emphasize the historical reliability of the New Testament. The New Testament writers are indeed out to win faith—but it is clear that they believe that they can do this simply by recounting, rather than distorting or inventing, the history of Jesus Christ.

Question: But don't the gospel accounts date from decades after the events they describe?

Yes. There may be as much as thirty years separating the crucifixion of Jesus and the writing down of Mark's gospel. But so what? The implication seems to be that they are inaccurate, or unreliable, because of this gap. But by the standards of the time, this is actually a very short gap. To make this point, let's look at the biographies we possess of someone else living at more or less the same time—the emperor Tiberius, who reigned from A.D. 14–37. Curiously, just as we depend primarily upon four gospels for our knowledge of the earthly life of Jesus, we are dependent primarily upon four biographies for our knowledge of Tiberius. One of these is clearly the work of an amateur, and is generally regarded as totally unreliable—and that is the earliest biography. The three most reliable biographies are those of Tacitus (dating from c. A.D. 115), Suetonius (dating from

c. A.D. 120) and Dio Cassius (written c. A.D. 230). Yet these were written between eight and 200 years after the death of their subject! The time lapse in the case of the gospels is small in comparison.

Anyway, we mustn't think that the gospel writers had to sit down decades afterwards and try to remember what Jesus said and did! Modern New Testament studies have emphasized that the period between Jesus' death and the writing down of the first gospel saw what Jesus said and did being passed down faithfully by word of mouth. Nowadays, of course, we are used to recording words in writing or on tape. We seem to have lost the ability to remember long stories. Yet, in the ancient world, long stories—like Homer's *Iliad* and *Odyssey*— were remembered and retold. If you read one of these nowadays, you would react with amazement if it was suggested that you memorize it and repeat it to someone else! They're just so long! But it was done regularly in the ancient world.

What we find in the gospels, then, are accounts of what Jesus said and did, passed down faithfully by word of mouth for about three decades, and then written down. As New Testament studies emphasize, we possess a remarkably reliable account of what Jesus said and did. Indeed, it is potentially superior to anything we have concerning the emperor Tiberius!

Question: Isn't Jesus just a good religious teacher?

Many critics of Christianity suggest that Jesus is simply a good religious teacher, like Socrates. Why, they ask, should they treat Jesus as being any different from them? Why should they listen to him, rather than any of the countless religious teachers in history? A

28

number of points can be made in response to this important objection.

1. Christians don't just think of Jesus as a dead rabbi

Of course Jesus was a religious teacher—nobody denies that. The question is whether he was *just* a religious teacher, or whether he was far more than that. It is impossible to read the gospel accounts of Jesus' ministry without being impressed by what he says. He taught with authority (Mark 1:27). But Christians have always regarded Jesus as being far more than a Jewish religious teacher, or rabbi. This is obvious from the way they talk about him. They talk about "being saved by Jesus," and refer to Jesus as "Lord," "Saviour" and "Redeemer." They may even refer to him as "God incarnate." The gospels themselves certainly present us with Jesus' teaching—but they focus far more than might be expected upon his death and what happened afterwards. Indeed, one respected New Testament scholar has suggested that Mark's gospel is basically an account of Jesus' death with an extended introduction!

2. We need more than just religious teaching if we're going to be saved

In his famous book *Mere Christianity*, C. S. Lewis makes an important point.

We never have followed the advice of great teachers. Why are we likely to begin now? Why are we more likely to follow Christ than any of the others? Because he's the best moral teacher? But that makes it even less likely that we shall follow him. If we can't take the elementary lessons, is it likely that we're going to take the more advanced one? If Christianity

29

only means one more bit of good advice, then Christianity is of no importance. There's been no lack of good advice over the last four thousand years. A bit more makes no difference.

You can see the point Lewis is making: we need more than someone who can just give us advice—we need someone who can change our situation.

St. Paul makes this point in Romans 7:17–25. There seems to be something about human nature which makes it want to do good, but prevents it from doing so. Something prevents us from doing the good things we'd like to. More than this, something seems to influence us to do things which we know are wrong. St. Paul identifies this "something" as sin, which he understands as a force working within us. And it's not just Christians who recognize that there is something wrong with human nature—many of the more serious attempts by atheists to understand the mystery of human nature end up speaking about "a fatal flaw" in our nature. Just telling us what is right and what is wrong doesn't help us, if there is something about us that prevents us from doing right and avoiding wrong! Yet Paul declares that Jesus Christ does far more than just teach us—he delivers us from the power of sin (Romans 7:24–25). He breaks the stranglehold of sin, and sets us free.

Let's take this point a little further. What's the point in telling people not to be frightened about death, if death really does mark the grim end of everything? But if someone could change that situation, could show us that death wasn't the end, or could assure us that anyone who believed in him would be raised from the dead— well, that would be something rather different, wouldn't it? And already we can see how important the resurrection is in connection with Jesus' relevance!

3. The resurrection points to Jesus being far more than just a good teacher

There has been no shortage of human religious teachers. The problem is deciding which ones to take seriously, and which to dismiss as cranks. At the time of the French Revolution, a whole series of new religions came into being, each with its own special teacher. Many thought that Christianity was a thing of the past, and so invented new religions to take its place. Yet none of them seemed to be able to capture the imagination of the general public. They attracted no followers, and most ended up collapsing after a few months or years. In desperation, one of the inventors of these new religions approached the great French statesman, Talleyrand. He asked how his religion could get off the ground. "My dear fellow," Talleyrand is supposed to have replied, "I suggest that you get yourself crucified and then rise again on the third day."

Only Jesus has ever been raised from the dead. The New Testament, of course, tells us about individuals (such as Lazarus: John 11:1–44) who were brought back from the dead by Jesus. Nevertheless, these individuals were brought back from the dead, only to die again. In the case of Jesus, we are dealing with someone who was raised from the dead, never to die again. Death's hold on him was completely broken. And the New Testament also emphasizes that Jesus was raised from the dead by God himself. Lazarus and Jairus' daughter may have been raised by Jesus—but Jesus himself was raised from the dead by God. Of course, your friends may not

31

believe that Jesus rose from the dead—and in the next chapter, we'll look at some of their difficulties. But the resurrection, if it really happened, immediately sets Jesus in a class of his own. He is unique. He is indeed a religious teacher—but he is far more than that. It is not wrong to say that Jesus was a great religious teacher: it is just inadequate. It doesn't go far enough. There is so much more that needs to be said! He is the risen Lord, who is able to encounter us, just as he encountered Paul on that road to Damascus. Here is no dead rabbi from the past, who now rots in some forgotten Palestinian grave—here is the living and risen Lord.

Question: Why do Christians believe in the divinity of Jesus?

Few people have any difficulty in accepting that Jesus was a man. The difficulties start with the belief that he is also God. The divinity of Christ is frequently challenged by critics of Christianity. Very often, it seems to be suggested that the first Christians rushed to the conclusion that Jesus was God, in order to give him added authority. The evidence, however, points in a rather different direction—that the first Christians were actually extremely reluctant to conclude that Jesus was God. After all, every Jew knew that there was only one God—suggesting that Jesus was God would have been a very difficult conclusion to draw. The only reason it *was* drawn was that the evidence in its favour was so overwhelming. For example, Thomas' famous declaration—"my Lord and my God!" (John 20:28)—was made only after he was absolutely convinced that Jesus really had risen from the dead. Let's look at the reasons underlying the characteristic Christian belief that Jesus is divine.

1. The New Testament often describes Jesus as doing things which only God can do

Let's look at an example. The Old Testament emphasized that God alone can save (see Isaiah 45:21–22). There was no saviour apart from God himself. Yet the New Testament talks about Jesus being our saviour (Acts 4:12; Hebrews 2:10). Jesus is the "Saviour; . . . Christ the Lord" (Luke 2:11). Titus 2:13–14 refers to "our great God and Saviour, Jesus Christ, who gave himself for us to redeem us from all wickedness." An especially interesting passage is Titus 1:3–4: verse 3 refers to God as "our Saviour," and verse 4 to Jesus Christ as "our Saviour." The implications of this passage are obvious and profound. You may already know that a fish came to be a symbol of faith for the early Christians—the five letters of the Greek word for "fish" (*ichthus*) were an acronym for "Jesus Christ, Son of God, Saviour." Here Jesus is clearly understood to do something which only God can do—save us.

Similarly, only God can forgive sins. Yet Jesus forgave sins. Mark 2:1–7 shows the outrage felt by the Jews when Jesus forgave the sins of a paralyzed man. "Son, your sins are forgiven"—and immediately, the Jews asked, "Who can forgive sins but God alone?" And they were absolutely right. None but God can forgive sins— yet Jesus did forgive sins. What are we to make of this? C. S. Lewis made this point forcefully in *Mere Christianity*:

Unless the speaker is God, this is really so preposterous as to be comic. We can all understand how a man forgives offences against himself. You tread on my toe and I forgive you. You steal my money and I forgive you. But what should we make of a man, himself unrobbed and untrodden on, who announced that he forgave you for treading on other men's toes and stealing other men's money? Asinine fatuity is the kindest description we should give of his conduct. Yet this is what Jesus did. He told people that their sins were forgiven, and never waited to consult all the other people whom their sins had undoubtedly injured. He unhesitatingly behaved as if he was the party chiefly concerned, the person chiefly offended in all offences. This makes sense only if he really was the God whose laws are broken and whose love is wounded in every sin. In the mouth of any speaker who is not God, these words would imply what I can only regard as a silliness and conceit unrivalled by any other character in history . . . I am trying here to prevent anyone saying the really foolish thing that people often say about him: "I'm ready to accept Jesus as a great moral teacher, but I don't accept his claim to be God." This is the one thing we must not say. A man who was merely a man and said the sort of things Jesus said would not be a great moral teacher.

By claiming to forgive sins, Jesus claims to be able to do something which only God can do.

2. The New Testament refers to Jesus in terms which imply that he is God

Three particularly important New Testament passages should be noted: John 1:1–18; Philippians 2:5–11; and Hebrews 2:9–18. You will find it helpful to read these along with a good commentary, which brings out the importance of each of the passages for our understanding of the full relevance of Jesus. Jesus is "the word become flesh." He is the one who humbles himself, taking upon himself human nature with all its

34

weaknesses in order to redeem us. He is Emmanuel,
"God with us."

There are also many other very important passages, of
which we can only note a few. For example, compare
Joel 2:32 with Acts 2:21. In his prophecy, Joel refers to
some period in the future when the Spirit of God will be
poured out on everyone, and when "everyone who calls
upon the name of the Lord will be saved." Now the
"Lord" in question is God himself. But Acts 2:21
understands this to be a reference to Jesus, whom God
has made "both Lord and Christ" (Acts 2:36) through his
resurrection from the dead (and notice the importance
of the resurrection in this connection). In other words, a
biblical passage which refers to God is understood by
the New Testament to refer to Jesus, on account of the
resurrection. Exactly the same thing can be seen hap-
pening in Philippians 2:10–11. Here Paul refers to
every knee bowing to the name of Jesus Christ—but he
is referring to an Old Testament prophecy (Isaiah 45:23)
which speaks of every knee bowing to God. There are,
of course, other passages which clearly imply the
divinity of Jesus—for example, John 20:28, in which
Thomas addresses Jesus as "my Lord and my God."
Hebrews 1:8 equates Jesus with God by quoting a
psalm addressed to God, and referring it to Jesus.

It may also be pointed out that many other New
Testament passages which don't actually state that Jesus
is divine certainly tend to point in that direction. It is
obvious that the New Testament regards Jesus as an
agent or representative of God, who had a unique
relationship with God. He showed us what God is like,
and was able to speak with divine authority (John 14:8–
14). When Jesus promised eternal life to all who believe

35

in him, we know that God stands behind that promise. The promise is made on God's behalf, and with God's authority. Jesus is understood to act as God and for God.

All these considerations clearly point to the conclusion that Jesus is God. We are not dealing with just one isolated piece of evidence which indicates this, but with the cumulative force of many pieces of evidence, all of which converge. The resurrection; what Jesus said; what Jesus did; what the first Christians believed about him—all these pieces of evidence, and others besides, have their part to play in building up to the crucial conclusion that Jesus is divine. It is a crucial conclusion, and the books suggested for further reading will help you justify and explain it to your friends. We now move on to consider the importance of this conclusion.

Objection: The idea that Jesus is divine is unnecessary

For some critics of Christianity, the divinity of Christ is quite unnecessary. If we didn't accept his divinity, a much simpler version of Christianity would result. It would be much simpler to understand and believe. Why bother believing in the divinity of Christ? As we saw in the last section, one important reason is that it is right! It may be difficult—but if it is right, we have little choice but to accept it. But some critics of Christianity seem to think that you can get rid of the idea of the divinity of Christ, and leave every other Christian doctrine intact. They seem to think it's like some sort of precision surgery, allowing you to remove apparently unnecessary parts of the human body (like the appendix), leaving everything else untouched. But in fact, removing the divinity of Christ from Christianity is like removing the heart from the human body—it's not taking away something unimportant, but the very source of its life and power! These words of C. S. Lewis sum up the situation perfectly: "The doctrine of Christ's divinity seems to me not something stuck on which you can unstick, but something that peeps out at every point so that you'd have to unravel the whole web to get rid of it." To deny the divinity of Christ is *unnecessary* and leads to a totally *inadequate* version of Christianity. Let's see what happens if we abandon belief in the divinity of Christ.

1. Suffering becomes an even greater problem

One of the difficulties which many people feel faces Christianity is suffering. God seems to stand aloof from the suffering of the world. It seems that God does not know what suffering involves. He seems to be distant from his world, uninvolved in its suffering. We suffer, while God does not. But for Christianity, Jesus is the suffering God incarnate. He knows and understands what it is like to suffer. God isn't like some general sitting in his bombproof bunker miles from the front line—he is one who has already fought in the same fight as his followers. This point is made with particular force by the playlet *The Long Silence.*

At the end of time, billions of people were scattered on a great plain before God's throne. Most shrank back from the brilliant light before them. But some groups near the front talked heatedly, not with cringing shame, but with belligerence.

"Can God judge us? How can he know about suffering?" snapped a pert young brunette. She ripped open a sleeve to reveal a tatooed number from a Nazi concentration camp. "We endured terror, beatings, torture and death!" In another group, a Negro boy lowered his collar. "What about this?" he demanded, showing an ugly rope burn. "Lynched, for no crime but being black!" In another crowd, there was a pregnant schoolgirl with sullen eyes. "Why should I suffer?" she murmured. "It wasn't my fault."

Far out across the plain there were hundreds of such groups. Each had a complaint against God for the evil and suffering he had permitted in his world. How lucky God was to live in heaven where all was sweetness and light, where there was no weeping or fear, no hunger or hatred. What did God know of all that man had been forced to endure in this world? For God leads a pretty sheltered life, they said.

So each of these groups sent forth their leader, chosen because he had suffered the most. A Jew, a Negro, a person from Hiroshima, a horribly deformed arthritic, a thaliodomide child. In the centre of the plain they consulted with each other. At last they were ready to present their case. It was rather clever.

Before God could be qualified to be their judge, he must endure what they had endured. Their decision was that God should be sentenced to live upon earth—as a man!

"Let him be born a Jew. Let the legitimacy of his birth be doubted. Give him a work so difficult that even his family will think him out of his mind when he tries to do it. Let him be betrayed by his closest friends. Let him face false charges, be tried by a prejudiced jury and convicted by a cowardly judge. Let him be tortured. At the last, let him see what it means to be terribly alone. Then let him die. Let him die so that there can be no doubt that he died. Let there be a host of witnesses to verify it."

As each leader announced his portion of the sentence, loud murmurs of approval went up from the throng of people assembled. And when the last had finished pronouncing sentence, there was a long silence. No-one uttered another word. No-one moved. For suddenly all knew that God had already served his sentence.

This playlet makes the point that God already knows what it is like to live upon earth as a man. He knows, and understands, what it means to be human. The whole problem of suffering takes on a new meaning, when we realize that God suffered in Jesus Christ.

2. We need more than just a good religious teacher

Throughout our long history, we have had lots of religious teachers. What good is one more? If Jesus is simply a man, he shares the common human problem—sin, suffering and death. If Jesus is just a human being, like us, then he's not the solution—he's part of the problem! What we need is someone who will change the human situation, not just tell us more about it. The Christian assertion that Jesus is God incarnate tells us that God has come into the world—that he has become involved with it. It changes our understanding of what God is like. It forces us to give up silly or inadequate views of God—like God being totally distant and remote, and unconcerned for his world. It forces us to give up inadequate views of Jesus—like Jesus being just a good religious teacher.

It tells us that Jesus is someone unique. He, and he alone among people, is God. It sets him apart from all other religious teachers. It gives weight to his teaching and actions. If Jesus is not divine, he's not the solution to the human situation—he's part of the problem. After all, religious teachers are just other human beings like us. They may be superior morally and intellectually but they are still merely humans. They can't change the human situation. And they view the human situation from the same standpoint as ourselves. They're in the same boat as the rest of us—and the boat seems to be going down.

But what if someone comes from outside the human situation? What happens if someone who knows what our situation looks like from God's viewpoint arrives? What if someone comes who sees us through the eyes of God? What if someone breaks down the wall of death? What if someone draws its sting? What if we are redeemed through the death of the Son of God on the cross? The insight that Jesus is God himself, that he is God incarnate, immediately identifies Jesus as being of enormous significance—because God himself has intervened in our situation in order to transform it. Jesus isn't part of the human problem—he holds the key to its solution. And that insight is only upheld adequately by belief in his divinity.

3. The cross no longer shows the love of God for us

Christianity has always insisted that the death of Jesus Christ on the cross shows the love of God for us. It is a very tender insight, one which is central to the Christian faith. Many people who have difficulty with the idea of the divinity of Christ have no difficulty with the idea of God's love being demonstrated in the death of Jesus Christ at Calvary. In fact, however, this invaluable insight depends in the first place upon Jesus' divinity. If Jesus isn't God, then his death shows nothing more than the love of one man for his friends. It is a demonstration of human, not divine, love. History is littered with people who have given their lives for their friends—what is so special about Jesus doing the same?

The only adequate answer is that Jesus was different.

He wasn't an ordinary man. This was no human act of love, but the love of God in action. In the tragic scene of Jesus Christ trudging towards his place of execution, we see none other than God himself, showing the full extent of his love for us to a wondering and disbelieving world. As Charles Wesley puts it in his great hymn *And can it be?*:

> Amazing love! how can it be
> That thou, my God, shouldst die for me?

To abandon faith in Christ's divinity is to lose forever the insight that the death of Jesus Christ shows forth the love of God for us. This just goes to prove the point C. S. Lewis made earlier—that the divinity of Christ underlies far more of the Christian faith than many people realize. It can't be eliminated without destroying the Christian faith. And there is no need to eliminate it, anyway!

It will be obvious that one major topic which has already been mentioned in this chapter is the resurrection itself. But many have difficulty with the idea of the resurrection of Jesus. In view of its importance, we will discuss some of these difficulties in the next chapter.

Questions for discussion

- Are the gospels reliable as history?
- Was Jesus just a good religious teacher?
- Is it important to uphold the divinity of Christ? If so, why?

For further reading

Craig Blomberg, **The Historical Reliability of the Gospels**. An excellent demonstration of the historical importance of the gospels. Very helpful reading!

Michael Green, **The Empty Cross of Jesus.** A very fine exposition of the relevance of the resurrection to our understanding of the importance of Jesus.

R. T. France, **The Evidence for Jesus.** A superb account of the evidence for the life and significance of Jesus.

Alister E. McGrath, **Understanding Jesus**, pp. 15–119. This book explores the New Testament evidence concerning Jesus, and explains the various ways of understanding the importance of Jesus Christ using helpful illustrations.

Stephen Neill, **The Supremacy of Jesus.** A very fine book, by a greatly respected writer, which explains why Jesus is totally different from other religious teachers.

Chapter 3

The Resurrection

The New Testament is dominated by the resurrection of Jesus. "He is risen!" is the theme which sounds again and again in its pages. It is the risen Lord who commissions his disciples, and sends them out to win all nations (Matthew 28:17–20). It was the risen Lord who encountered Saul on the road to Damascus. It is the same risen Lord whom we know and experience.

"But," a critic might say, "I am not really sure that the resurrection happened in the first place. In fact, I'm not really terribly sure what you mean by the word 'resurrection' anyway." In this chapter, we'll be looking at some of the genuine difficulties people have with the resurrection of Jesus Christ, and how you can help them with these.

Objection: It was easy for first century Jews to believe in a resurrection

"Look," your friend might say, "it was easy for those first Christians to accept the idea of Jesus' resurrection.

They lived in the first century. They expected things like resurrections to happen. My problem is that I live two thousand years later, when we just don't expect things like that to happen. I find it very difficult to accept, I'm afraid."

Now this is a perfectly understandable difficulty. In response, you can argue along two lines. First, your friend is wrong about first century Jewish beliefs. Second, the behaviour of the disciples around the time of the crucifixion clearly indicates that they weren't expecting Jesus to be raised from the dead so soon afterwards.

1. Jewish beliefs about the resurrection

Your friend is actually wrong on one crucial point—those first century Christians didn't expect Jesus to be raised at all. Perhaps they ought to have expected this—after all, Jesus foretold his coming death and resurrection as he and his disciples went up to Jerusalem for the last time (see Mark 8:31; 9:31–32). Nevertheless, the idea of someone being raised from the dead here and now—in human history! —was outrageous at the time! One widespread expectation was that people would be raised from the dead at the end of time—on the "last day." Look at John 11:23–24. Martha summarizes this resurrection expectation very neatly: it is something which happens at the end of time—not something which could happen there and then. But others at the time, such as the Sadducees, denied any resurrection altogether (Mark 12:18; Acts 23:8).

After two thousand years, Christians are more used to the idea of Jesus being raised from the dead—but the idea is actually very strange. Indeed, by the standards of the first century, it was an extraordinary belief. It was totally different from the two opinions in general circulation—that there was no resurrection, or that there would be a general resurrection right at the end of time. Paul was able to exploit the differences between the Pharisees and Sadducees on this point during an awkward moment in his career (see Acts 23:6–8). But this belief concerned the future resurrection of the dead, at the end of time itself. The idea of somebody being raised from the dead here and now, and appearing to witnesses, was unheard of.

The Christian claim was that Jesus had been raised now, before the end of time. When Paul refers to Jesus as the "firstfruits" of the resurrection (1 Corinthians 15:20–23), he means that he was the first of many to rise from the dead—but that Jesus had, indeed, been raised before anyone else. This is quite different from Jewish ideas about the resurrection. So there was something quite distinct and unusual about the Christian claim that Jesus had been raised from the dead, which makes it rather difficult to account for.

Why should all the first Christians have adopted a belief which was so strange by the standards of their time? The first Christians simply didn't adopt a widespread Jewish belief, as some have suggested—they altered it dramatically. What the Jews thought could only happen at the end of the world was recognized to have happened in human history, before the end of time, and to have been seen and witnessed by many. This is a startlingly new belief, and its very novelty raises the question of where it came from. Why did the first Christians adopt this belief? The event of the resurrection of Jesus, it would seem, caused them to *break with* (not echo!) traditional beliefs concerning the resurrection. Neither of the two beliefs of the time bear any resemblance to the resurrection of Jesus.

It is easy for us to overlook how strange, how offbeat, the Christian proclamation of the resurrection of Jesus seemed to the first century. The unthinkable appeared to have happened, and for that very reason demanded careful attention. Far from merely fitting into the popular expectation of the pattern of resurrection, what happened to Jesus actually contradicted it. The sheer novelty of the Christian position at the time has been obscured by two thousand years' experience of the Christian understanding of the resurrection—yet at the time it was wildly unorthodox and radical.

2. The disciples weren't expecting Jesus to be raised

This point about the *unexpectedness* of Jesus' resurrection is confirmed by the behaviour of the disciples around the time of the crucifixion. It is obvious from the gospel accounts of the crucifixion of Jesus that the first disciples thought that this was the end of everything. The man who they'd given up everything to follow was executed. The men who executed him were professionals: to suggest that they made a botched job of killing Jesus (so that Jesus revived in the tomb) is terribly implausible. We can feel a profound sense of sadness as we read those gospel accounts. The disciples slink away, demoralized and dispirited. They give every impression of being hopeless and helpless, like sheep without a shepherd.

And then suddenly all this changes. A band of sad demoralized cowards is transformed into a joyful group of potential martyrs, for whom death no longer holds any terror. Something which they didn't expect has obviously happened. How else can we account for this remarkable transformation? A mass delusion, perhaps? Hypnosis? The alternatives are certainly there but they lack any real plausibility. As Pinchas Lapide, a leading Jewish scholar, has perceptively remarked in his work *The Resurrection of Jesus,* "without the resurrection of Jesus, after Golgotha, there would not have been any Christianity." This Jewish writer comments thus on the changed mood of the disciples:

> When this scared, frightened band of the apostle which was just about to throw away everything in order to flee in despair to Galilee; when these peasants, shepherds and fishermen, who betrayed and denied their master and then failed him miserably, suddenly could be changed into a confident mission society, convinced of salvation and able to work with much more success after Easter than before Easter, then no vision or hallucination is sufficient to explain such a revolutionary transformation.

Let's illustrate this further by looking at Peter. Peter was the man who failed Jesus when the going got tough. When Peter seemed to be in personal danger through being associated with Jesus before the resurrection, he denied having anything to do with him (Mark 14:66–72). But, as far as we know, Peter was martyred at Rome for his faith after the resurrection (John 21:18–19 refers to this). The change is obvious and remarkable. What has caused Peter to abandon his fear of death? Perhaps the finest answer to this question is provided by Peter himself: it is the "new birth into a living hope through the resurrection of Jesus Christ from the dead" (1 Peter 1:3).

Throughout the New Testament, we find the theme of

47

victory over death proclaimed with great enthusiasm. It was something relevant, something exciting, something liberating. Christians need not fear persecution nor death itself, because death has been defeated through the resurrection of Jesus. Now it is *possible* that the first Christians were a crowd of deluded idiots, who were prepared to be martyred for a myth—but somehow, that doesn't seem very likely. It is obvious that something totally unexpected happened to Jesus and that this transformed the situation of those first Christians.

Before his death, Jesus spoke to his disciples about the future. He told them that he would suffer, be rejected, be killed and that finally he would be raised again after three days (Mark 8:31). He told them that, after his death and resurrection, he would go before them to Galilee (Mark 14:28). It seems that the disciples found these words difficult to understand. "Being raised again"—what could that mean? After all, everyone would be raised on the last day. How could Jesus talk about being raised again and then going to Galilee? It just didn't make sense.

Now when the disciples were faced with the empty tomb, it seems as if scales suddenly fell from their eyes, as they realized that these words were being fulfilled. Suddenly they seem to have realized that Jesus wasn't talking about a resurrection right at the end of time, but here and now—on the third day. Suddenly, all the pieces of the jigsaw seem to have come together, giving a picture of Jesus' resurrection which differed completely from anything they had expected! The disciples weren't expecting Jesus to be raised—hence their initial amazement and fright, and their subsequent joy, as they realized what must have happened. Once more, we find clear evidence for the unexpectedness of Jesus' resurrection.

So the suggestion that it was easy for the first Christians to believe in Jesus' resurrection because they were expecting something of the sort is based upon a misunderstanding. You should have little difficulty in explaining this along the lines suggested.

Objection: All this nonsense about the resurrection makes a simple gospel complicated

"Look," your friend might say, "it seems to me that Christianity is basically about the teaching of Jesus. In other words, Jesus is a good teacher, like Mohammed or Socrates. Now that I can accept. But why do you go and make this simple gospel so complicated by all this nonsense about the resurrection? It makes Christianity much more difficult to accept!"

Once more, this is an important objection. It must be taken seriously, partly because it reflects a serious misunderstanding about what Christianity really is. Your basic answer which we'll be justifying in a moment would be something like this.

"Well, I believe in the resurrection because it seems to me that there is no other way of explaining the evidence. I can understand your difficulty, but I think the only criterion we can use here is not whether it is *easy to believe,* or whether it's *simple,* but whether it is *right.* And if it *is* right, then the idea that Jesus is just a good teacher (like Socrates) has to be abandoned as inadequate. It just doesn't take account of what the resurrection means. The resurrection places Jesus in a unique category: there's never been anyone like him before, and there never will be again. He's unique and

49

the reason why he's unique is that the resurrection proves that he's the Son of God."

Now there's a lot in that response, all of which is important. Let's look at the points.

1. The real question is whether the resurrection really happened or not—not whether it makes Christianity too complicated!

2. If the resurrection took place, it establishes Jesus as unique.

3. If the resurrection took place, Jesus is far more than a good religious or moral teacher: he's the Son of God.

Simplicity is one thing; truth is quite another! As C. S. Lewis pointed out, the really simple religions are actually those *invented* by human beings.

Question: What is the New Testament evidence for the resurrection of Jesus?

The main lines of evidence from within the New Testament for the resurrection of Jesus are the following.

1. The tomb was empty

Each of the four gospels tells us that the tomb in which Jesus' body was laid on the Friday evening was empty on the Sunday morning (Matthew 28:1–10; Mark 16:1–8; Luke 24:1–11; John 20:1–8). There is a certain degree of difference between the four accounts on minor points. Was the tomb discovered just *before* dawn (Matthew and John), or just *after* dawn (Mark)? Matthew, Luke and John mention that the women, after realizing that the tomb was empty, told the other disciples, but Mark makes no mention of this fact. Yet all the gospels insist upon a core of hard historical fact:

1. The tomb was empty.
2. Jesus appeared to his disciples and others after his death.
3. The Jewish authorities couldn't disprove the Christian claim that Jesus had been raised from the dead.

Variation on minor points of detail is a characteristic feature of eyewitness reports. If you ever listen to witnesses in a courtroom, you will very often be amazed by the different way in which they describe the same event. They may all be able to agree on what happened, and when. But on minor points of detail (for example, what happened immediately before or after that event), they very often differ. An event is experienced differently by various people. Major agreement is accompanied by minor disagreement. Look at the way in which the same events are reported by different news networks on television, for example. Minor discrepancies in details of eyewitness reports actually point to their authenticity, not their inauthenticity. If the gospel accounts of the resurrection were based upon an invention, we would have expected their minor disagreements to have been removed before publication! Let's take this point a little bit further.

Critics of the New Testament resurrection accounts often seem to apply one set of standards to the New Testament, and a totally different set to their everyday existence. For example, if the *Washington Post* and *New York Times* reported the same story in slightly different terms, hardly anyone (except a New Testament critic who applied his standards consistently!) would dream of suggesting that one had copied the other. Similarities between the stories would be held to arise from the event they were reporting. It is only in the world of New Testament criticism that stories are never derived from events, but simply from other people's versions of that story. And nobody would draw the ridiculous conclusion that, because their accounts were so similar, the event they reported could not have happened! The world of New Testament critics sometimes seems to be one in which similarities between reports of an event are enough to allow them to conclude that the event did not happen.

Let's suppose that all four gospels reported *exactly* the same pattern of events on that first Easter Day, perhaps down to using the same words. Would that make them more credible to a critic? Certainly not! He would immediately argue that they were fabrications. They were cooked up. He would suggest that the accounts had been "doctored" to bring them into line with each other! He would dismiss them as crude forgeries. On the other hand, if they differed wildly from each other, the same critic could dismiss them with equally great ease but for different reasons. He would argue that they weren't talking about the same thing. He would suggest that it was impossible to gain any impression of what had really happened. He would dismiss them as having no importance in assessing the claim that Jesus Christ had been raised from the dead.

So, totally different or totally identical accounts would be dismissed by such a critic. What, then, would such a critic accept as reliable? The answer can only be accounts which vary on minor points, but are agreed upon the central point of importance—which is exactly what we find in the gospel accounts of the discovery of the empty tomb! All agree that the tomb was discovered to be empty early on that Sunday morning, and that there was universal astonishment at this event (which, of course, further backs up the suggestion that they weren't expecting a resurrection).

Another point is interesting. In Matthew 23:29–30 we find reference to the practice of "tomb veneration." When a prophet or martyr died, his tomb became a place of worship for his followers. But the New Testament contains not so much as a hint that Jesus' tomb was venerated. Why should the first Christians not have treated Jesus' tomb with the respect it would normally have been given? There was clearly something *odd* about Jesus' tomb, if we are to account for this unlikely omission. Jesus' tomb never became a place of pilgrimage, or even of interest, to Christians. And the empty tomb accounts for this omission with ease: as Jesus was raised from the dead, there was no point in venerating his tomb! He wasn't there any more.

Of course, a critic might say, this is all very well but you've just been talking about the gospels. What about Paul? We don't find any reference to an empty tomb in Paul's writings, do we? And of course he is right. But so what? Why should we expect to find any such reference in Paul's writings? Let's make three points.

First, as mentioned earlier, Paul is writing *letters*, not accounts of the life, death and resurrection of Jesus Christ! When I write letters to Christian friends about the faith we have in common, I concentrate upon the relevance of the risen Christ for our lives. And that's what Paul is doing. He has no need to talk about the empty tomb.

Second, Paul was not a witness to the empty tomb. He could certainly witness to the power of the resurrection to transform his life—but not to something which he had not seen personally. Equally, his witness to the resurrection of Jesus rested upon his personal experience (1 Corinthians 15:8).

Third, Paul's letters tend to deal with matters on which he and those he was writing to *disagreed.* Usually, Paul has to intervene to settle some dispute or other. He has no need to dwell on matters on which they agree (although he occasionally does). The empty tomb was not a matter of disagreement among the first Christians, and Paul simply has no need to refer to it. Paul never refers to the fact that Jesus taught in parables. He never refers to the fact that Jesus was condemned before Pontius Pilate. He doesn't need to! But this doesn't allow us to conclude that Jesus *didn't* teach in parables, or that he *wasn't* condemned before Pontius Pilate. The argument from Paul's silence on the matter overlooks both the nature of Paul's writings, and the reason why he wrote them in the first place!

However, Paul's emphasis upon the resurrection in his writings is beyond dispute. While still a persecutor of the Christians, Paul encountered the risen Lord on the road to Damascus (see Acts 9:1–9; 22:4–16; 26:9–18; Galatians 1:11–16). His faith ultimately depended upon that encounter with the risen Lord—how could he doubt that he was risen? Indeed, he often spoke of the "power of the resurrection" (Philipians 3:10). And there were others who had shared the same experience—Paul mentions that there were more than 500 witnesses to this experience (1 Corinthians 15:5–7), many of whom were still living twenty-five years after the resurrection. And it was the resurrection which convinced Paul that

Jesus really was the long-awaited Messiah (Romans 1:3–4).

In short: the evidence is that the tomb was empty. The question which had to be answered was simply this: why?

2. The corpse of Jesus could not be accounted for by other means

It is of the greatest importance that the New Testament does not contain so much as the slightest trace of an attempt to reconcile belief in Jesus' resurrection with the existence of his corpse in some Palestinian grave. Nor is there any hint—in the New Testament, or anywhere else—that the Jewish authorities either produced, or attempted to produce, the body of Jesus. Had this been done, the preaching of the early church would have been discredited immediately. Was there no enemy of the first Christians who could have destroyed their preaching of the resurrection by that one simple and dramatic act—the production of the body?

But the intriguing fact remains that no such move was made to discredit the first Christians' proclamation of the resurrection and its implications—and the simplest explanation of this remarkable omission is that the corpse was disquietingly absent from the tomb. All the evidence indicates that the tomb was empty on the third day. The controversy at the time concerned not the *fact* of the empty tomb, but the *explanation* of that emptiness. Matthew records one explanation advanced by one group of critics of Jesus—the disciples had stolen the body at night (Matthew 28:13–15). But it is clear that the disciples believed in a somewhat more exciting explanation—that Jesus had been raised from the dead.

Once more, we must emphasize this point: there can be no doubt that the first disciples did believe that Jesus had been raised by God. The reports concerning the empty tomb are completely consistent with this belief, and must be regarded as being at least as historically plausible as any report of any event from the time. Our task is simply to account for this belief, and ask whether it is likely to be correct.

It would have been a simple matter to discredit the Christian message. It could have been done at a stroke. All that was needed was one body. The Christian message could not have survived if the corpse of Jesus had been on public display in Jerusalem. The Christian assertion that Jesus had been raised from the dead was potentially very threatening to two groups of people—the Jews and the Romans. It was in the interest of both to discredit this assertion immediately if they could. But they couldn't, and they didn't. Why not? All the evidence points to the disconcerting fact that Jesus' corpse could not be found.

3. Jesus was worshipped as God

The next point which must be considered is the remarkably exalted understandings of Jesus which became widespread within Christian circles within a surprisingly short period after his death. As we have already seen, Jesus was not venerated as a dead prophet or rabbi—he was worshipped as the living and risen Lord. At some points in the New Testament, as we noted in the previous chapter, Jesus appears to be explicitly identified with God himself, and some sort of implicit identification along these lines is widespread, and would become normative in the following centu-

56

ries. In his letter to Trajan, which we also noted in the previous chapter, Pliny refers to the Christian practice of singing hymns to Jesus as God.

Furthermore, as we saw earlier (pp. 34–38), at several points in the New Testament words originally referring to God himself are applied to Jesus. Two examples are especially interesting. In Romans 10:13 Paul states that "everyone who call upon the name of the Lord [Jesus, in this case] will be saved"—yet the original of this Old Testament quotation (Joel 2:32) is actually a statement to the effect that everyone who calls upon the name of God will be saved. In Philippians 2:10 Paul alters an Old Testament prophecy that everyone will one day bow at the name of God (Isaiah 45:23) to refer to Jesus.

But how could this remarkable transformation in the perceived status of Jesus have come about? He died as a common criminal, perhaps even a prophet, or maybe a martyr—but the most this would merit would be veneration of his tomb (see Matthew 23:29). Of course, we have already noted that there was a problem about Jesus' tomb, which was found to be empty so soon after his death. But the point still remains important: why did the early Christians start talking about a dead rabbi as if he were God? And, perhaps even more interesting, why did they start talking about him as if he were alive, praying to him and worshipping him?

Once more, we must note that it is possible that they were the victims of a hysterical delusion which has continued to this day. But there is another far more convincing explanation—that they believed that Jesus had been raised from the dead by God, thus establishing or demonstrating the unique relationship between God and Jesus. And it was on the basis of their understand-

57

ing of this unique relationship that the early Christians based their views of Jesus.

Your friends may well have the idea that Christians look to Jesus as a teacher in much the same way as Marxists look to Marx. But, as we saw in the last chapter, this just isn't right! You need to explain to them that Christians don't treat Jesus as a dead figure from the past who had some interesting ideas. They worship him as the living Lord. Jesus isn't treated as a dead rabbi—even a super-rabbi!—but as someone who is present, who is *alive,* who can meet us here and now.

Objection: The resurrection can be explained on other more rational grounds

"Surely," your friend might say, "we can explain the resurrection accounts of the New Testament in other ways. The idea of Jesus being raised from the dead is difficult for me to accept. There must be a simpler explanation of what happened—perhaps there was some misunderstanding on the part of the disciples. Perhaps they were dishonest. Or maybe they were just deluded idiots, who got confused about what happened."

The main alternative explanations of the resurrection accounts of the New Testament are the following.

1. Jesus didn't really die at all on the cross—he just fainted, and later he revived.

2. The first Christians "borrowed" pagan myths about dying and rising gods. Let's look at these individually.

1. Jesus didn't really die upon the cross

Is it really likely that experienced Roman executioners would have botched Jesus' execution? Would they have been likely to confuse fainting and dying? Some nineteenth century rationalists certainly thought so, and their ideas have even found their way into more recent discussions of the subject. Here's the theory that one of them—H. E. G. Paulus, writing in 1828—put forward.

In first century Palestine, it was quite common for people to be buried when they weren't actually dead. And this is exactly what happened with Jesus. He fainted on the cross (see John 19:34). But Paulus is well versed in the latest medical theory (in 1828 that is). He knows that one way to make someone recover is to bleed them. And what really happened was that the spear didn't penetrate Jesus' heart, but simply cut a vein. The loss of blood then helped him recover from his trance.

Jesus' body was then taken to a grave. The smell of the spices in which he was wrapped, and the coolness of the tomb, combined to revive him. So, on the Sunday morning, he was able to leave the tomb. Fortunately, the great stone which had blocked the entrance had been moved by an earthquake, so he was able to get out without too much difficulty. And nearby he managed to find a set of gardener's clothes, which he put on (and, of course, Mary then mistook him for a gardener: John 20:15).

After that, Jesus put in the occasional appearance to his disciples. These disciples, of course, being unsophisticated and backward peasants, thought that he was risen from the dead. After forty days, however, he realized that he was finally going to die from his wounds. So he climbed a nearby mountain to say goodbye to his followers. A cloud then appeared from somewhere, so that Jesus disappeared from view. Then

Jesus went off somewhere—nobody knows where—never to be heard of again, and died.

Without wishing to seem disrespectful, this seems very difficult to take seriously. The possibility that a group of professional Roman executioners should have failed in their task is improbable enough. The reference to "blood and water" when Jesus' side was pierced after the crucifixion (John 19:34) would seem to be a reference to separation of the blood into clot and serum, indicating that Jesus was unequivocally dead. As this presumably wasn't a known medical fact when John's gospel was written, it is unlikely to have been included to make the account seem more plausible. We are also being asked to believe that this hungry, thirsty and seriously wounded man would have been able to unwind his grave-clothes and crawl from his tomb. And not only that, but we are being asked to believe that he would have given his disciples the impression that he was the conqueror over death, when in fact he was obviously a seriously ill man who would die of his wounds shortly afterwards!

Now it is possible that someone who is deliberately determined not to believe in the resurrection may find this a convincing explanation. Even many critics of Christianity, however, find it totally implausible, saying little for the credibility of those who suggest it. It is just not an adequate explanation.

2. The resurrection is based on a myth

This is a more subtle and sophisticated objection, which you are much less likely to meet. However, you may come across it, in which case it is important that you know what to say in response. If your friend is into ancient Egyptian mythology, he might well suggest that the idea of dying and rising gods was commonplace in the ancient world. Gods such as Attis, Adonis, Isis and Serapis were originally deities. The Egyptians, noticing that vegetation kept disappearing in winter and reappearing in spring, developed the idea that there was some sort of vegetation god who spent six months on high and six months on earth. Later, under the influence of Greek thought, these gods came to be thought of as dying and rising again, in a yearly cycle. And so, your friend might argue, all that Christians have done is to hijack these myths. They have taken the idea of a god who dies and rises again, and based the idea of the resurrection upon it.

This suggestion might well have been taken very seriously between about 1890 and 1930. Since then, however, scholarship has moved on considerably. The parallels between the pagan myths of dying and rising gods and the New Testament accounts of the resurrection of Jesus are now regarded as remote, to say the least. For instance, the New Testament documents record with some care the place and the date of both the death and the resurrection of Jesus, as well as identifying the witnesses to both. The contrast with the ahistorical narrative form of mythology is striking. *When* did Attis die? *Where* did he die? *Who* saw it happen? *When* did he rise again? *Where* did he rise again? *Who* were witnesses to this alleged "resurrection?" The New Testament gives us answers to all six of these questions. It treats the resurrection as a definite historical event. But the "dying-and-rising-god" myth makes no claim to be based in historical reality.

Furthermore, there are no known instances of this

myth being applied to any *specific historical figure* in pagan literature, so that the New Testament writers would have given a stunningly original twist to this mythology. It is at this point that the wisdom of the great literary scholar C. S. Lewis—who actually knew something about myths—must be acknowledged. Lewis realized that the New Testament accounts of the resurrection of Jesus bore no relation to real mythology, despite the protests of some theologians who had dabbled in the field in a thoroughly amateur fashion.

Another theory which was in fashion in the 1930s was that Christians took over what are sometimes known as "gnostic redeemer myths," which also spoke of a dying and rising saviour god. Since about 1950, however, it has been generally accepted that the gnostic redeemer myths—which the New Testament writers allegedly took over and applied to Jesus—were to be dated from later than the New Testament itself. The gnostics, it seems, actually took over Christians ideas! Anyway, there is no evidence whatsoever that the first Christians knew anything about Egyptian mythology. How could Christians adapt something of which they knew nothing? The first people to proclaim the resurrection of Jesus were mostly Jewish peasants, who would hardly have come across such sophisticated foreign mythological speculation.

The idea that the resurrection is based upon some ancient eastern myth is not taken with any degree of seriousness in scholarly circles today. You may still, of course, find the occasional student who has read some influential book from the 1920's—like J. G. Frazer's *Adonis, Attis, Isiris*—and takes its ideas seriously. But scholarship has moved on since then! Whatever the resurrection may be, it isn't a rehashed Egyptian myth!

Objection: Dead people don't rise again

"But," your friend may say, "surely I am right to exclude the possibility of the resurrection? Dead men don't rise. Jesus was a man. Therefore Jesus cannot have risen from the dead—and that's all there is to it. There is just no point in arguing about the evidence—because you can't have evidence for something which is an impossibility!"

This is a classic objection, which picks up some themes developed by the eighteenth century Scottish philosopher David Hume. Hume argued that you needed contemporary analogues for events like the resurrection. In other words, you need to be able to point to comparable events in the present before you can believe in the resurrection. Because we don't see dead men or women rising from the dead today, Hume argued, we have reason to call into question whether Jesus rose from the dead in the first century.

This argument sounds convincing, until we begin to look at it more closely. Let's suppose that about one person in a thousand rose from the dead on a more or less regular basis. It's a common occurrence. We've all seen it happen. The idea doesn't present any difficulties for us. And so we would have no difficulty in accepting that Jesus rose from the dead in the first century.

But if this was the case, we would not have any interest in Jesus! Jesus would simply be yet another example of something we all know from experience. He wouldn't be special. His resurrection wouldn't be *important.* The fact that he was raised from the dead wouldn't distinguish him from all others.

Now the simple fact is that Christians have always insisted that Jesus was unique—that he was singled out from all others by the fact that he, and he alone, was raised from the dead in history. There will be a general resurrection at the end of time, certainly—but Jesus is the only person ever to have been raised from the dead in human history. Lazarus was brought back to life, only to die again: As we noted earlier, the resurrection of Jesus is different. He is the "first-fruits from the dead" (1 Corinthians 15:20). In other words, his resurrection is unique and without any parallel in human history.

This obviously raises a difficulty. If—as Christians have always insisted is the case—Jesus' resurrection is unique, then by definition there can't be any other occurrences of the same event. If there were other occurrences, it would certainly make it a lot easier to believe in Jesus' resurrection—but his resurrection would no longer have the crucial importance which Christians attach to it.

The fact that there are no other persons who have been raised from the dead may well make it more difficult to accept that Jesus was raised—but it also underscores Jesus' uniqueness. He, and he alone, was singled out in this way. He was not merely special—he was unique. What is it that distinguishes Jesus from Socrates, Mohammed or Gandhi? None but Jesus was raised from the dead by God—and it is *this* which leads us to take Jesus' teaching with the seriousness it deserves. After all, if you suspect that you are dealing with the Son of God, you will take his teaching more seriously than you might otherwise! For the New

64

Testament, Jesus' resurrection clinches his identity—it proves that he was the Son of God (Romans 1:3–4 is worth noting here). It is the key to his identity and relevance.

In this chapter, we've been looking at some of the main objections which might be raised by your friends against the resurrection of Jesus. None of them is fatal. By helping them to see this, you may be able to remove obstacles which prevent them from encountering the risen Christ. And that encounter itself is the final proof of the resurrection!

Questions for discussion

- What are the main lines of evidence for the resurrection in the New Testament?
- What does the empty tomb prove?
- What would happen to Christianity if belief in the resurrection was abandoned?

For further reading

Michael Green, **The Empty Cross of Jesus,** pp. 91–123. An excellent discussion of the various objections to the resurrection, and how they can be handled.

Michael Green, **The Day Death Died.** A splendid and very readable study of the resurrection and its relevance today.

Alister E. McGrath, **Understanding Jesus,** pp. 63–80. A summary of the New Testament evidence for the resurrection, and its importance for our understanding of Jesus.

Chapter 4

Salvation

The idea of salvation is central to the gospel. The New Testament exults in the fact that, through the death and resurrection of Jesus Christ, God has made salvation available for us. As a study of any of the works listed for further reading at the end of this chapter will show, there is a tremendous richness to the Christian understanding of the cross of Christ which there just isn't room to discuss here. What we are going to look at instead is a number of specific difficulties people have in thinking and talking about salvation which need careful consideration. The present chapter will deal with five major problem areas.

Question: What is salvation?

For many people, the very idea of salvation is something of a problem. "What do you mean by 'salvation'?," they may ask. "What does it mean to be saved?" It is very helpful to be able to explain the various ways in which Scripture describes salvation, in order to help people get a "feel" for what it is like. The biblical understanding of what Jesus Christ achieved upon the cross is remarkably rich and profound. It can challenge and excite people—but it needs to be *explained*. So far in this book, we've been looking at ways in which you can defend Christianity against objections. In this chapter, we're mainly concerned with explaining what Christianity has to say on the great question of the relevance of the death of Jesus Christ for the human race. We begin by explaining how Christians understand what "salvation" actually means.

The New Testament uses a number of ideas to explain what Jesus Christ achieved on the cross. So deep and rich is the Christian understanding of what he achieved that no one single idea can capture it in its totality. So the New Testament uses a series of ideas and images to describe it. Just as a group of jigsaw pieces build up to disclose an overall picture (which no single piece can disclose by itself), so these ideas and images build up to give us a full understanding of what Jesus achieved on the cross. Let's look at the main ones and see how you might explain them.

1. Salvation

The very name "Jesus" means "God saves" (Matthew 1:21), showing how important the idea of "being saved" or "salvation" is within the New Testament. What does it mean? The Greek word used (*soteria*) has two main meanings, each of which is very helpful in explaining the relevance of Jesus Christ's death and resurrection for us.

First, it means "being rescued," or "being delivered from a dangerous situation." For example, you might be

67

in prison, or held captive by a foreign power (just as Israel was held captive in Egypt). When you are "saved," you are set free from bondage. You are liberated. Human beings are held captive by the power of sin and by the fear of death. These are forces which have enormous influence over our lives. Christ came to die and rise again in order to release us from these forces. He came that we might have life in all its fullness, through breaking the power of sin and death over us.

Second, it means "making whole" or "restoring." If you compare some translations of the New Testament, you'll find that Mark 5:34 is sometimes translated as "your faith has saved you" and sometimes as "your faith has made you whole." There is a very close connection between the ideas of "salvation" and "wholeness" or "healing." For the Christian, "salvation" includes the very important idea of "being restored to wholeness." Through Christ's death and resurrection, we are offered the possibility of being fulfilled as persons. Our potential as human beings can only be fully realized when we come to enter into a relationship with God. The French philosopher Pascal remarked that "there is a God-shaped gap within us"—meaning that we are incomplete until we relate to God. The story of creation in Genesis (Genesis 1:26–27) emphasizes that God created us in his image and likeness—in other words, with the capacity to relate to him. The cross and resurrection of Jesus opens up the possibility of being restored to the fullness of our relationship with God. We are made whole again by being restored to fellowship with God. Salvation is about being rescued from the power of sin and the fear of death—and about being restored to fellowship with the living and loving God.

Many people are concerned about their "human potential"—in other words, about how to live fully as human beings. Even secular humanists regard this as an important question. And it is important that the Christian contribution to this discussion be heard. For Christianity is also about fulfilling the human potential, although the solution it provides will differ from that of secular humanism. The gospel proclaims that Jesus Christ came in order that we might have life in all its fullness, by opening the way to restoring us to fellowship with God. That fullness, of course, has both personal and social implications: Christians must never behave as if salvation is simply concerned with individual believers: God has a vision for the salvation, the making whole, of society as well.

This point about the social dimension of salvation is important. Critics of Christianity often suggest that it's just about "pie in the sky when you die." In other words, it's just about saving individuals. The scriptural idea of "salvation," however, takes in two major themes: first, restoring the individual to fellowship with God, and second, restoring human society to what God wishes it to be. It's about the restoration of both human beings and society to what God intended them to be. "Restoring the kingdom" embraces both individual and society. To suggest that the Christian gospel is just about saving individual souls is a serious distortion of what Christianity is about. Christianity has a great social vision, which its critics often manage to overlook, even though Christians have been in the forefront of many great social reforming movements.

Where, then, do Christians differ from other social reforming movements? Perhaps most importantly in their understanding of human nature. The idea of "original sin," which I'll discuss shortly, points to there being something flawed in human nature. Many social movements, such as Marxism, argue that there is something wrong simply with *society:* change society, and all will be well. The Christian suggests that there is something inherently flawed in human nature, which is reflected in the way society has developed. It is human nature, as much as society, which needs to be restored. The Christian vision is comprehensive, embracing both individuals and society: *both* need restoration to wholeness.

2. Reconciliation, forgiveness

Many of the ideas—including the two we're going to look at now—used by the New Testament to show the relevance of the death and resurrection of Jesus Christ are based upon personal relationships. The parable of the Prodigal Son (Luke 15:11–32) is perhaps one of the best-known passages of Scripture. It is an ideal starting point for explaining the ideas of "reconciliation" and "forgiveness" to your friends. It is a powerful way of beginning to explore the meaning of the death and resurrection of Jesus Christ.

The parable tells of the transformation of a personal relationship—a personal relationship which has gone wrong. It tells us of how the son becomes alienated from his father. He decides to go his own way, into the "distant country" (Luke 15:13). While he is far from his father, he realizes just how much the relationship meant to him. He decides to return home, and ask for his father's forgiveness. And so he begins the long journey home, wondering how his father will react to his homecoming. When he is still a long way from home, his father sees him and runs to meet him. He has been waiting for him! And so the rejoicing begins.

This parable beautifully illuminates the situation in which many young people find themselves. Like the prodigal son, they have wandered into a "distant country," where they thought they would be free and happy. Yet life without God so often seems meaningless and unsatisfying. The far country seems very attractive, seen from a distance—but once they get there, they find it fails to meet up to expectations. They long to return home. Every day and age has its own special "distant country." For one generation, it may be the seductive delusion of a Marxist utopia; for another, existentialist philosophy; for a third, narcotics. Each seems attractive. They seem exciting and new, compared with the constancy of Christianity. And then the dreadful moment comes, when the illusion is shown up for what it really is. And perhaps then they begin to think about God. Is he there? Is he interested in them? And would he be prepared to have them?

It is questions such as these that the ideas of "reconciliation" and "forgiveness" begin to deal with. The New Testament tells us that our relationship with God is rather like other personal relationships. All of us are involved in personal relationships of one sort or another, and can immediately understand the gospel proclamation when it's presented in these terms. Let's suppose that two people (let's call them "Paul" and "Elizabeth") develop a relationship. They come to mean a lot to each other. And then Elizabeth does

71

something to offend Paul. Perhaps Elizabeth doesn't even realize that Paul has been offended. But the relationship goes wrong. Paul and Elizabeth become alienated from each other. The relationship is in ruins.

Then Paul decides to do something about the situation. He decides to talk to Elizabeth and confront the fact that the relationship has gone wrong. He will explain how much the relationship means to him, and offer to forgive her. This means that Elizabeth will have to admit that she has hurt Paul, and face up to all the pain and hurt it has caused—but having done this, the relationship is restored. Paul and Elizabeth are reconciled to each other.

You could use analogies like these to begin to explain the cross to your friends. The New Testament tells us that God takes the initiative in trying to restore our relationship with him. The full extent of our separation from him is shown. We realize that we, like the prodigal son, are in a "distant country," far from God. We realize that we are sinners. And then we begin to appreciate the full extent of God's love for us, as we realize that the Son of God died for us upon the cross (John 3:16; Romans 5:8; Galatians 2:20). God deals with the objective reality of sin through his death on the cross, breaking its stranglehold upon us. The death of Jesus Christ upon the cross demonstrates the reality of our sin and the full extent of our separation from God—and at the same time speaks to us of the overwhelming tender love of God for us. We realize how much we mean to God. And then perhaps we feel moved to do something about it.

The cross speaks to us of reconciliation and forgiveness. For St. Paul, "God was reconciling the world to himself in Christ" (2 Corinthians 5:19). Elsewhere, he uses the same word to refer to the reconciliation of a husband and wife whose relationship has broken down (1 Corinthians 7:11). Through the death and resurrection of Jesus Christ, God is making possible our reconciliation to him. Our relationship with him can be transformed. All the obstacles to that relationship have been removed by God. One only remains—our reluctance to repent, to say "yes" to his offer of forgiveness. God may seem far away and distant—but that can change, and change very suddenly. He is offering us forgiveness, allowing us to set the past behind us, in order to go forward with him into eternal life.

3. Justification

For Paul, Christians have been "justified through faith" (Romans 5:1). But what does the word "justification" mean? For some people, "justification" is something you do to righthand margins on word processors—it hasn't got anything obvious to do with God! However, the word has the basic meaning of "putting in the right." Sin is a wrong relationship with God—but faith is a right relationship with God. To be "justified" means that we are placed in a right relationship with God—or, to put it another way, we are made "right with God." Through the death and resurrection of Jesus, we are enabled to be "right with God" (Romans 4:24–25; 5:1 GNB).

Question: What is "sin?"

The word "sin" itself can cause considerable difficulty for some people. Many people have problems with Christianity because they don't understand what "sin" actually means. They think it has something to do only with sexual morality. It's therefore useful to be able to explain the basic scriptural ways of talking about sin. Two main meanings are of particular use in helping us to explain the idea of sin.

1. Sin as missing the mark

Just as an arrow misses its target by falling short, so we have missed our full relationship with God by falling short of the required standard. "All have sinned and fall short of the glory of God" (Romans 3:23). Of course, some may come closer to the target than others, but the fact remains that they still missed it. "A miss is as good as a mile," as they say. Some people are much more moral than others—but they still fall short of the required standard.

2. Sin as rebellion

Deep down in human beings is a desire to go one's own way, to be independent of God. The story of Adam and Eve (Genesis 3:4–6) tells of how Adam decided he wished to be like God, being able to decide what was good and what was evil—in other words, to set himself up in the place of God. And the prodigal son rebels against his father, setting off into the "distant country" to be independent. Just as children rebel against their parents, so the New Testament speaks of us rebelling against God. We want to live our lives without him.

One of the most poignant passages in Scripture is Hosea 11:1–5. Here God speaks of his overwhelmingly tender love for his people: he brought them out of Egypt and tended them. Yet his people now seem to have forgotten all about him. They want to live their lives

74

without taking any notice of the God who loved them and brought them out of captivity into the promised land. Sin is living one's life without God—and time and time again, Scripture speaks to us of the hurt that this causes to God. After all, God loved the world so much that he sent his only Son to die for us. Imagine the hurt and grief it must cause him to be overlooked. The cross shows how heartbroken God is on account of us. This way of thinking about sin helps us understand the problem of sin (living without God), while also reminding us of the incredible depths of the love of God for us.

A helpful distinction which you can make when explaining Christianity to your friends is between *sin* and *sins*. Sin is like a disease, whose symptoms are sins. In other words, sin is what is wrong with human nature, and sins are the effects of this problem. Christianity is primarily concerned with sin—with the basic problem of human nature. It identifies sin as a force, a power, which exercises influence over us. Before we can stop sinning, its power needs to be broken. It is like an illness which makes us commit sins. Before we can stop sinning, we need to be cured of this illness. For St. Paul, the gospel is about God's intervention to deal with sin. Through the death and resurrection of Jesus Christ, the power of sin is broken. Christ's death and resurrection are like a drug which combats the illness of sin, gradually healing us of its wounds. The gospel deals with the root cause of sins: it doesn't just tell people to stop sinning, but deals with the problem which makes them want to sin in the first place.

Many people find the idea of "original sin" especially difficult. One way of explaining this idea is particularly helpful. The doctrine of original sin tells us that we are born into the world alienated from God. Or, to put it another way, we are born into the world cut off from God. God seems far away and distant, so distant that he might as well not exist. We don't do something which causes us to be cut off from God, because we are already alienated from him. Perhaps you have read the Nobel Laureate William Golding's novel *Lord of the Flies*, a story about what happens to a group of young boys stranded on a desert island paradise. Yet already within them, the boys have the seeds of the evil which unfolds in the pages of the book. Golding vividly explores what he calls "the darkness of man's heart," as he shows that there is already some force within us, working for evil, from our youth upwards. *Lord of the Flies* is a very helpful way into a discussion with students of English literature on the problem of original sin and the Christian answer to it.

The doctrine of original sin prevents anyone from thinking that our natural relationship with God is right or good enough. It points to there being something wrong with us—some distortion or bias in our nature, some darkness in the depths of our being which we cannot deal with by ourselves. It tells us just how far we have to go if we are to relate to God properly and have life in all its fullness. It is only when we realize just how far we are from God that we begin to appreciate just what good news the gospel really is. The doctrine of original sin destroys any illusions we may have about our standing before God. "Unless a man is born of water and the Spirit, he cannot enter the kingdom of God" (John 3:5). To relate to God properly and fully, we need to be born all over again (John 3:3). Our physical birth must be followed by a spiritual birth, if we are to have life in all its richness and fullness.

Earlier, we looked at the biblical idea of "reconciliation" as one way of unpacking the full meaning of the death and resurrection of Jesus. Sin is about being alienated from God. Like the prodigal son, we are in a "distant country." God seems to be far away and remote. The gospel, however, proclaims that we can be reconciled to God—that through the death and resurrection of Jesus Christ, the way back from the "distant country" to the waiting father has been opened up. Original sin is about alienation from God—just as the gospel is about reconciliation with God through the death and resurrection of Jesus Christ. Original sin is the "before," and salvation the "after."

I hope that these brief comments about salvation and sin will help you begin to think of ways of explaining how the death and resurrection of Jesus is of relevance to your friends. We shall return to discuss how you can help them see the relevance of the cross and resurrection soon. First, however, we need to look at a genuine difficulty you may encounter in talking about salvation.

Objection: Isn't everyone saved anyway?

This is the position often referred to as "universal salvation," or sometimes just "universalism." The New Testament often affirms the universal saving will of God. God "wants all men to be saved and to come to a knowledge of the truth" (1 Timothy 2:3). As God wants everyone to be saved, some argue, this proves that everyone eventually will be saved. Why, then, bother talking about Christianity or salvation?

This is an important question and there are a number

of answers you can give. For example, it is perfectly obvious that the New Testament works on two basic assumptions: first, that God does indeed want everyone to be saved; second, that not everyone will be saved. The New Testament makes a distinction between those who are going to be saved and those who aren't. A more helpful way of dealing with this question, however, is to get your friend to think through the implications of his suggestion that everyone will be saved.

The gospel affirms the love of God for sinners. Time and time again, we find the New Testament writers exulting in the love of God. Paul asks the Ephesian Christians to try to "grasp how wide and long and high and deep is the love of Christ" (Ephesians 3:18). But what is love? Love is basically about one person freely offering himself or herself to another. Now as everyone who has ever been in love is only too painfully aware, falling in love with someone doesn't always mean that they automatically fall in love with you! They have a say in whether or not they fall in love with you as well! You can tell them how much you love them. You can do all sorts of things to try and prove how much they mean to you. But in the end, it's a simple fact of life that your offer of love may be turned down. The fact that you love someone doesn't force them into loving you.

Now let's return to God. God loves us. He goes to incredible lengths to show just how much we mean to him. On the cross, we can see the supreme demonstration of the love of God for us—God gave his only Son, so that whoever believes in him should not perish, but have everlasting life (John 3:16). And it is also obvious that God would very much like us to love him as well. But we are given the enormous privilege of saying "no" to that love. God does not force himself upon us: he offers himself to us. He knocks at the door of our life, asking us to open the door—but he doesn't break that door down and force his way in. Perhaps you know the famous picture by Holman Hunt, *The Light of the World*. This picture shows Jesus, carrying a lantern, gently knocking at a door, seeking admission from the occupant. He doesn't stand there with a sledge hammer, preparing to smash the door down and gain admission without the occupant's permission.

The gospel proclaims that God loves us, and very much wishes us to accept his offer of love and be saved. But the ball is in our court. God has firmly but courteously done everything he could to gain for us our salvation, and he is now offering it to us. But he does not force us to accept his gift. Universalism, however, is obliged to assert that God forces us to be saved.

If all are to be saved, then the possibility of not being saved is excluded. Universalism may well suggest that Jesus knocks at the door of our life, seeking admission— but what happens if we don't want to let him in? Perhaps it is at this point that the sledge hammer is brought out! God may use the velvet glove at first—but the iron fist comes out if we refuse to be saved. And universalism conjures up the most appalling view of God—that of a tyrant, who has no concern whatsoever for the wishes of his creatures. Their God-given freedom is overruled. They *must* be saved, whether they like it or not. This is totally removed from the view of God which we find in the pages of the New Testament.

Christianity asks us to think of a God who loves us so much, that he gave his Son to die for us. Like the father awaiting the return of the prodigal son, he respects the freedom and choice of those whom he loves. Universalism asks us to think of a God who rapes us—who rides roughshod over our wishes in order to force himself upon us. Unlike the father in the parable, perhaps he sends out troops to recapture the prodigal son, forcing him to return in chains against his will. It is unthinkable and gains no support from the New Testament. God does indeed desire that everyone will be saved—but the New Testament affirms that it is up to us to respond to that offer of salvation. God respects us. Universalism is quite simply sub-Christian, perverting these most precious insights concerning the love of God for sinners.

Question: How is "salvation" relevant?

The New Testament develops at least three major ways of interpreting the cross and resurrection of Jesus, each of which is charged with enormous relevance for the human situation. You will probably find that at least one of these three ways of looking at the cross will challenge your friends.

1. The cross as the forgiveness of sins

Many people have a deep sense of personal inadequacy and guilt. "How," they may ask, "can someone like me ever enter into a relationship with God? After all, he's so holy and righteous, and I am so sinful and wretched." This is a very important question, and you need to appreciate that Christianity has a very powerful answer to give.

The cross demonstrates God's determination to deal with human sin. It shows just how serious and costly a thing real forgiveness is—and reassures us that our sins really have been forgiven. God doesn't say something like, "Never mind, let's pretend that sin doesn't exist." Instead, God brings together in the cross of Jesus his total condemnation of sin and his tender love for the sinner. We see in the death of Jesus on the cross the full impact of human sin, the full cost of divine forgiveness, and the full extent of the love of God for sinners. God hates the sin and loves the sinner. Christ endured the cross for our sakes; and bore the full penalty for sin. As a result, sin is forgiven—really forgiven. We are able to come to God as forgiven sinners, as men and women whose sin has been condemned and forgiven. We must learn to accept that we have been accepted by God, despite being unacceptable.

So the cross is indeed good news to those who feel that they could not possibly come to God on account of their sin or inadequacy. The gospel gloriously affirms that God has forgiven that sin, has overcome that inadequacy. The words of 1 Peter 2:24 are very helpful and important here: "He himself bore our sins in his body on the tree, so that we might die to sin and live to righteousness; by his wounds you have been healed." Through the great events which centered on Calvary, God has wiped out our past sin and, at enormous cost, given us a fresh start. He has smoothed out every difficulty in order that we might go forward with him into eternal life. We are able to turn our backs on our past (which is what the idea of "repentance" basically means) in order to go forward into the future with the God who loves us.

2. The cross as victory over death

Many people are frightened of death. Contemporary existentialist philosophers point out how humans try to deny death, try to pretend that they aren't going to die. We like to think that death is something which happens to somebody else. It is very difficult for us to come to terms with the fact that our personal existence will one day be terminated. It is a very threatening and disturbing thought. People are afraid of death. How often has it been said that death is a forbidden subject in the modern world?

It is here that the gospel has a decisive contribution to make. The New Testament points to the death and resurrection of Jesus Christ as God's victory over sin and death (1 Corinthians 15:55–56). Christ "shared in their humanity so that by his death he might destroy him who holds the power of death–that is, the devil— and free those who all their lives were held in slavery by their fear of death" (Hebrews 2:14–15). The gospel invites those who are afraid of death to look at what God has achieved through the cross and resurrection of Jesus. So long as human beings walk the face of this earth knowing that they must die, the gospel will continue to be relevant and powerful. We must never lose sight of the relevance and power of the gospel here!

3. The cross as a demonstration of the love of God for sinners

It is natural for us to feel lost in the immensity of the universe. We need to feel loved, to feel that we are important to someone else. Yet at the root of the lives of many, there is a virtual absence of any meaning. President John F. Kennedy once remarked that "modern American youth has everything—except a reason to live." And the words of Jean-Paul Sartre express this point with force: "Here we are, all of us, eating and drinking to preserve our precious existences—and yet there is nothing, nothing, absolutely no reason for existing." We could even give a name to this feeling of meaninglessness—we could call it an "existential vacuum." But that doesn't solve the problem. Many still feel lonely and lost, in a vast universe which threatens to overwhelm them.

It is this feeling of meaninglessness which is transformed through the electrifying declaration that God— the same God who created the universe—loves us. Love gives meaning to life, in that the person loved becomes special to someone, assumes a significance which he otherwise might not have. Christianity makes the astonishing assertion—which it bases upon the life, death and resurrection of Jesus Christ—that God is profoundly interested in us and concerned for us. We mean something to God; Christ died for us; we are special in the sight of God. Christ came to bring us back from the "distant country" to our loving and waiting father (but not to force us to go with him, as universalism suggests—only to invite us to accompany him back, if we wish to). In the midst of an immense and frightening universe, we are given meaning and significance by the realization that the God who called the world into being, who created us, also loves us and cares for us, coming down from heaven and going to the cross to prove the full extent of that love to a disbelieving and wondering world.

Question: Why is a response to the gospel necessary?

One final problem remains. Some people find it difficult to understand why they need to respond to

God's offer of salvation. They find it difficult to accept that they need to *do something* to enter into a full relationship with the loving and living God. Surely, they might say, it is enough simply to admit the truth of the gospel? It is therefore helpful to be able to explain the need for a response on our part. Four main ways of doing this should be noted.

First, imagine that someone is offering you a gift. They hold out their hand, and offer you that gift. It is there, waiting for you to accept it. But until you reach out and take it, it will not be yours. The offer is genuine—but you must respond to it. As the great theologian John Calvin remarked, faith is like an empty open hand, stretched out towards God, waiting to receive from him. You need to receive, to accept, the great gift of salvation which God is offering you, if it is to be yours. Faith is basically saying "Yes!" to God and accepting that salvation and making it our own.

Second, think of the idea of reconciliation. We have already seen how this is an important New Testament way of understanding what God has done for us through the death and resurrection of Jesus Christ. Now imagine that Paul and Elizabeth, whom we met earlier, have fallen out again. Their relationship is in ruins. However, Elizabeth decides to try to restore their relationship. She goes to Paul, and explains how much the relationship means to her. She offers to be reconciled to him, so that their relationship can be restored. What happens if Paul refuses to respond to her offer of reconciliation? The relationship remains ruined. It is only by accepting her offer of reconciliation that the relationship is restored to its fullness. So it is with God. God offers us reconciliation, through the death and resurrection of

Jesus Christ. But unless we accept that offer, our relationship with God remains unchanged.

Third, think of the idea of forgiveness. The idea is, of course, central to the gospel. What happens if God offers us forgiveness, yet we refuse to accept it? Is the relationship transformed? To accept an offer of forgiveness is actually quite difficult. It means admitting that we need forgiveness, that we have done something which has hurt someone else. It means having to apologize. The biblical idea of "repentance" is of central importance: it means acknowledging the hurt we have caused to another, admitting that we are at fault, and humbly asking for forgiveness. But it also means restoring a relationship. Not accepting an offer of forgiveness means that the relationship is unchanged. It is only by accepting God's offer of forgiveness that our relationship with him is transformed. Of course our need for repentance is difficult for us to admit—for the prodigal son, it meant getting up, going to his father, and saying, "Father, I have sinned and am no longer worthy to be called your son." But it also means coming home to a loving and waiting God, who rejoices at our return.

Fourth, think of the gospel as being like a medicine. We have already seen how salvation can be understood as healing. When penicillin was discovered, it was hailed as a wonder drug, capable of curing illnesses (like blood poisoning) which had once been fatal. If you had blood poisoning, you could now be cured—provided you took penicillin. The drug could not cure you unless you took it. The gospel is like penicillin—it is capable of transforming our situation. But it must be taken. We need to make a response to the gospel, by applying it. To acknowledge the *truth* of the gospel without responding to it is like saying that penicillin could cure your illness—without taking it! You recognize its potential—but don't benefit from it. A person dying of blood poisoning doesn't gain much from the knowledge that his illness *could* be cured by penicillin—he needs to take it, and *be* cured!

All these illustrations make the same point. It is an obvious point but one which some people have genuine difficulty in grasping. You need to accept God's offer of forgiveness. You need to say "Yes!" to God. You need to apply the gospel. You need to do something. There are, of course, a number of ways of explaining this "something" to your friends. You may suggest they think of reaching out to receive a precious gift which is being offered to them. You may suggest that they think of accepting an offer of forgiveness. You may suggest that they think of opening a door which leads into their lives (Revelation 3:20). You may suggest that they think of eating the bread of life (John 6:48), or drinking the water which gives eternal life (John 4:13–14).

One of the difficulties in explaining the gospel in very simple terms, as I have tried to do throughout this book, is that there is a danger of oversimplification. It will be obvious that pressure on space has meant that I have not had time to discuss the role of the Holy Spirit in salvation. For example, the Holy Spirit is actually involved in our response to God—even before we say "Yes!" to God, the Holy Spirit has been at work within us, prompting us to make this response. There is, of course, a long-standing debate within Christianity upon the nature and extent of the role of the Holy Spirit in conversion, which it is impossible to go into at this point. It is not, however, a debate which need trouble you as you try to explain Christianity to your friends. All are agreed that a response is necessary to God's offer of grace and forgiveness, and it is this aspect of the matter which is of prime importance to you in your discussions with your friends.

Questions for discussion

■ How would you explain the meaning of the following ideas to interested friends: redemption; adoption?
■ How would you explain the idea of sin?
■ Does God's wish that everyone should be saved mean that all must be saved?
■ In what ways are the death and resurrection of Jesus Christ relevant to the needs of modern humanity?

For further reading

Alister E. McGrath, **Understanding Jesus,** pp. 123–184. A careful discussion of the various ways of thinking about the idea of "salvation," and explaining it to your friends.
I. H. Marshall, **The Work of Christ.** An excellent discussion of what Christ achieved upon the cross.
J. I. Packer, **Evangelism and the Sovereignty of God.** A useful examination of the relation of God's sovereignty and human responsibility. Although it mainly deals with the question of evangelism, its relevance to the question of universal salvation will be obvious.
John Stott, **The Cross of Christ.** A masterly discussion of the importance of the death and resurrection of Jesus Christ in relation to our salvation. Exceptionally thorough and very stimulating.

Chapter 5
God

Inevitably, you are going to want to talk about God to your friends. And here you may encounter a cluster of objections which it is helpful to be able to meet. There are four main areas of difficulty, which we'll explore individually.

Objection: God doesn't exist anyway

You will very often find yourself immediately confronted with an objection which goes something like this: "Maybe it was easy for people to believe in God a thousand years ago—but nowadays it's impossible. God's existence has been disproved." In fact, this is just not the case. Whether you're a Christian, and believe that God *does* exist, or an atheist who believes that he *doesn't*—your position is a matter of faith, not fact. God's existence can neither be conclusively proved nor disproved. In the end, both the atheist and the Christian take their positions as a matter of faith.

This point is important, as most atheists and agnostics

will probably be prepared to admit the *possibility* (however slight!) of God's existence. Their difficulty often lies in accepting that the existence of God is actually relevant to them. God's existence cannot be *disproved* conclusively, as we shall show in what follows. Once the possibility of God's existence is conceded, the argument will take a very different direction. You can then begin to explain some of the reasons why Christians believe in God—for example, by asking what happened at the resurrection, and what its implications are (see chapter 3). The further reading suggested at the end of this chapter will be helpful in this connection.

Nevertheless, you are likely to encounter people who feel that God's existence can indeed be disproved. The two most common arguments often used as "disproofs" of the existence of God are frequently encountered, and we're going to look at both.

1. *God is just some kind of wish-fulfillment*

This theory has an interesting intellectual pedigree, going back to the Hegelian writer Ludwig Feuerbach in the 1830s, and being developed by Sigmund Freud in the early twentieth century. The argument goes something like this. Human beings basically want God to exist. Now, as Voltaire once said, "If God didn't exist, it would be necessary to invent him." And what Christians have done is to invent God. The human longing for the existence of God is projected onto an imaginary heavenly screen. God is a sort of wish-fulfillment: he isn't really there but Christians imagine that he is because they want him to be there. You have probably heard this sort of idea being discussed already. There are three main responses which you can make.

First, this is not a proof that God doesn't exist—it's simply an assertion that he doesn't. It's a hypothesis, a theory, and certainly not an established fact! Sigmund Freud's explanation of religious belief, for example, is still regarded by some people as having discredited Christianity—yet it is evident that Freud's allegedly "scientific" approach to Christianity is hopelessly influenced by outdated nineteenth-century rationalist presuppositions. The issue has been prejudged, not scientifically studied.

Second, it appears to rest upon a rather basic logical mistake. The argument seems to go like this:

Premise 1. The fact that we want something to exist doesn't mean that it does exist.
Premise 2. We want God to exist.
Conclusion. Therefore God can't exist.

But the conclusion doesn't follow from the premises! Let's suppose that you want a large milk shake after a really tedious lecture. Obviously, the fact that you want one doesn't mean that one will exist for that very reason! On the other hand, it doesn't mean that one cannot exist, just because you happen to want it! Whether you want something or not actually has no direct bearing on whether it exists or not.

Anyway, you could develop this argument in a most uncomfortable manner.

Premise 1. The fact that we don't want something to exist doesn't mean that it doesn't exist.
Premise 2. Atheists don't want God to exist.
Conclusion. Therefore God exists.

90

The same basic logical error is still being made—but this time the boot is on the other foot! This time it is atheism, it is being suggested, which is indulging in "wish-fulfillment." Atheists don't want God to exist—and therefore they invent his non-existence to support their wishes! The "wishful thinking" argument can cut both ways. It is not particularly difficult to think of people who have very good reasons for wishing that God doesn't exist—for example, the commandant of a Nazi extermination camp, who is hardly likely to view his future judgment with much enthusiasm. For such a person, belief in the non-existence of God is unquestionably wishful thinking. Does it therefore follow that God *does* exist for this reason? Certainly not!

The great Christian writer C. S. Lewis, however, suggested that the fact that many people feel some deep desire for God, which no physical thing could ever satisfy, does actually point to the existence of God. Lewis pointed out that human feelings of need (like hunger and thirst) point to the means by which they could be satisfied (by food and drink). Why, he asked, should not the same thing be true of our spiritual hunger and thirst? Do not they point to the means by which they can be satisfied? Lewis' famous sermon "The Weight of Glory" develops this point with great force, and would be particularly interesting to any studying in the field of literature.

Thirdly, you could point out that this alleged "disproof" of God's existence seems to work on the assumption that the existence of God guarantees you some sort of easy ride through life. God is seen as some sort of spiritual consolation, who makes life more bearable for you. Now it is certainly true that a relationship with God

91

does alter our entire outlook on life. But what, you might ask, about the martyrs? What about those who felt that God was asking them to give up their lives for his sake, or asking them to do things which were most uncomfortable? The first Christians often ended up getting martyred for their faith—and if that faith was just some sort of consoling thought to help them cope with life, it's very difficult to see why they should have ended up suffering and giving their lives in the name of "consolation!" Perhaps there is a danger that some sort of "wish-fulfillment" might underlie faith, at least for some Christians—but the suggestion that it underlies the faith of *all*, or even *most*, Christians is not to be taken too seriously.

In the end, the idea of God as a "wish-fulfillment" is an interesting hypothesis, lacking any experimental foundation or proof, which seems to rest upon a basic logical error. The Christian can hardly be expected to give up his faith in God on the basis of such a flimsy argument.

2. *The Marxist critique of Christianity*

This is one of the more influential criticisms of Christian faith you are likely to come across in student circles. In view of this, we shall spend some time dealing with it. Curiously, however, most students seem remarkably ignorant of what Marx actually said. You may well find that your friends who argue that Marx has "disproved" Christianity have the most superficial acquaintance with what Marx actually said. In fact, Marx's criticism of Christianity has no bearing on whether God exists or not—or, indeed, upon *any* major Christian doctrine. Let's examine this criticism.

Marx argues that religion (and he makes no attempt to

distinguish the various religions) comes about through the human social and economic situation. Religion arises from a specific social and economic situation, and in turn supports that situation. For Marx, any social and economic system which is basically capitalist will inevitably produce religion as a means of comforting those who are oppressed (thus diverting their attention from revolution) and justifying the position of those who rule. Religion is "the opium of the people," consoling the workers in their unjust situation, and also diverting their attention from the present world. Religion prevents social change.

Marx then develops these ideas further. If the social and economic situation can be changed, there will no longer be any need for religion. Religion is basically the result of unjust social conditions: when the revolution comes, these conditions will be overthrown, and religion will simply disappear of its own accord. Marx's theory of the "historical inevitability of socialism" (no longer, incidentally, regarded as correct by most social scientists) points to Christianity and all other religions fading away as socialism gradually gains the upper hand. There will no longer be any need for it. The communist revolution will eliminate the causes of religion, and thus it will simply disappear. Let's use Marx's own terms: religion is a symptom of socio-economic alienation within capitalism—so that if you remove this alienation through the communist revolution, religion will become superfluous.

We are now in a position to begin responding to this criticism of Christianity. The most important response concerns the way in which Marx handles Christianity.

Marx never seems to make the slightest attempt to

deal with the truth-claims of Christianity. For Marx, religion is wrong (because it delays the revolution and supports the ruling classes): as Christianity is a religion, it is wrong for that very reason. This, however, is a distressingly inadequate analysis of Christianity. Marx's materialism leads him to dismiss any concept of a spiritual realm, including the existence and relevance of God. "Religion" is just a social phenomenon, having no contacts with a reality lying beyond the material world. Marx seems to feel that you can dismiss the truth of a religion because that religion gets in the way of his vision of a communist society. Where is there any indication that Marx has shown that a basic Christian belief—for example, the resurrection—is *wrong?* The only substantial criticism which Marx can level at Christianity is that it gets in the way of his vision of a socialist society. It is inconvenient, perhaps—but it remains to be shown that it is wrong.

This point is of central importance in responding to the Marxist critique of Christianity. However, certain other points might be made. For example, Marx seems to base some of his criticism of Christianity upon his experience of the role of some of the Christian churches in nineteenth century Europe. Marx correctly noted that these churches tended to support the status quo, and generally lent their support to the ruling classes of their day. Marx seems to have drawn from this observation the conclusion that Christianity universally supports oppression. Marx's criticism of "Christianity" is important, in that it demonstrates how easy it is for Christian churches to become too closely linked with the establishment—but it is not a fundamental criticism of Christianity itself. It is not an essential feature of the

Christian faith that it *should* be linked with the social establishment.

Marx may legitimately challenge the Christian church at this point, reminding it of its need to foster just social conditions. Furthermore, the Christian church should listen to his criticisms, and attempt to respond to them. His criticisms apply to the Christian church, however, rather than to Christianity—in other words, to Christian institutions rather than the Christian faith. They apply primarily to the way in which Christianity is applied. Marx persistently seems to think that Christianity can be identified with the medieval papacy or the Protestant church-state establishment of the nineteenth century. He criticizes the manner in which Christianity is applied, rather than Christianity itself. But he has not gone even the slightest way towards "disproving" any Christian doctrine, let alone the existence of God.

Another point may be made here against the Marxist analysis of religion. There is a very obvious and serious contradiction between experience and theory here. Religion should, according to Marx, have died away in communist societies. In fact, there is no evidence that this has happened. In an effort to make theory and reality come together, certain communist societies attempted to suppress Christianity by force: this, however, has now been generally recognized as counterproductive. It also seems to suggest a certain lack of faith among Marxists in their analysis of the causes of religion: why the need to forcibly suppress something which should naturally fade away? Marx's analysis of the causes of religion would certainly seem to require revision.

Although Marxism now gives every indication of

being in decline, it still represents an important way of understanding the world which seems to exercise considerable attraction in student circles. It is for this reason that it is important to understand its basic ideas. One of the most penetrating studies of Marx's critique of Christianity is by the highly respected German writer Hans Küng. In his famous work *Does God Exist?*, Küng concludes:

> Marx never seriously came to terms with the biblical understanding of God and man and with the message of Jesus Christ and consequently was not at all familiar with the "social principles of Christianity" (he was even inclined to think that the first Christian communities practised cannibalism when they met for the eucharist). Hence, in his presentation, Christianity appears as a power ideology, determined purely by economic and social interests, with a church subordinated to the state, justifying all injustice in the here and now with an illusory promise of happiness in the hereafter. What is properly and specifically Christian remained alien to Marx throughout his life.

Your responsibility is to ensure that modern student Marxists are presented with a reliable version of "what is properly and specifically Christian," and that students influenced by the Marxist critique of Christianity are made aware of its weaknesses.

Question: How can I believe in God when I see such suffering and pain in the world?

For many people, suffering is an obstacle to faith. "How can I believe in God," they ask, "when I see so much suffering in the world?" This question tends to be asked for two very different reasons. First, your friend may find this an intellectual difficulty. Second, your friend may have seen a relative suffer, or experienced considerable suffering, and thus find it an emotional

96

difficulty as well. It is helpful to work out which of these two situations your friend is in, as it may affect what you say to them.

Let's begin by outlining some points you could make to someone who finds suffering an intellectual difficulty.

1. The existence of pain and suffering was not thought to be a reason for not believing in God until the seventeenth century. The respected philosopher Alasdair MacIntyre (once a Marxist-inclined atheist, now a Christian) argues persuasively in his famous work *The Religious Significance of Atheism* that "the God in whom the nineteenth and twentieth centuries came to disbelieve had been invented only in the seventeenth century." People knew all about pain and suffering before then—but they didn't regard them as calling God's existence into question! Only recently (since the Enlightenment) have they been seen as doing this. What has changed? The facts—or the way we look at them? The facts are much the same as they always have been—but it is only recently that the existence of pain and suffering have been seen as calling God's existence into question. Might this difficulty not be due simply to a change in intellectual fashions?

2. Is there any reason for supposing that God could have created a world in which there was no pain and suffering? David Hume, the great Scottish philosopher, pointed out that we couldn't claim that the world we know is "the best of all possible worlds," as we didn't have any other worlds to compare it with! But for the same reason, we can't say that there could be a *better* world. We may well feel that this world could have been put together in a different way, thus avoiding suffering and pain—but in the end we just can't prove this.

3. We can't blame God for all suffering and pain. As C. S. Lewis remarks, "It is men, not God, who have produced racks, whips, prisons, slavery, guns, bayonets, and bombs." Equally, it is largely through human greed that poverty and starvation arise. As relief agencies emphasize there is more than enough food in the world to prevent starvation: the problem arises through the greed of those who have more than enough.

4. Suffering is not just a difficulty for Christianity! There is no religious or philosophical system, except one, which can explain the problems of suffering and evil. The exception is "dualism," which sees a permanent conflict between the forces of good and evil. Dualism has no difficulty with suffering or evil: they arise through the great battle that is going on between the good and the evil gods, as they wrestle for control of the world. Pain and suffering are caused by the actions of the evil god. This neatly explains the problem of suffering and evil—but at what a high price! The idea of "dualism" brings with it a whole range of new problems, as C. S. Lewis so persuasively demonstrated in *Mere Christianity!* But are we to dismiss all these great religious and philosophical systems, simply because there is one difficulty they all share?

For those who find suffering more of an emotional difficulty, the following points may be helpful.

1. Suffering and pain are a problem because they seem to call God's goodness into question. They suggest that he may not be quite the good and loving God we thought he was. Yet against, this, we have to set God's total commitment to our well-being and ultimate salvation which we can see in the cross. "God so loved the world that he gave his one and only Son" (John 3:16).

The Son of God himself suffered and died for us. Is it conceivable that the God who loved us so much should turn against us? Martin Luther, the great German reformer, felt that the only way of dealing with the problem of pain and suffering was to think about Christ dying upon the cross. In his pain and suffering we see the Son of God working out our salvation. He went through that pain and suffering for us. A quotation from a former Archbishop of Canterbury, William Temple, makes these points very well.

> "There cannot be a God of love," men say, "because if there was, and he looked down upon the world, his heart would break." The church points to the cross and says, "It did break." It is God who made the world," men say. "It is he who should bear the load." The church points to the cross, and says, "He did bear it."

2. It cannot be emphasized too strongly that God does not will suffering upon us. Let's explore this point. Creation involves risk. Imagine two parents, lovingly bringing a child into the world. He means everything to them, and they love him dearly. They do everything that they can for him. They explain to him about good and evil. And then the child grows up, and rebels against his parents. He becomes addicted to cocaine, and in his desperate search for enough of the drug to meet his addiction, he ends up robbing and killing. Were the parents responsible? In one sense, yes—after all, they brought the child into this world. But in another, they are obviously not—they did all they could to guide him into the right course of life. They loved him, and did all that they could for him. Even now—with their son branded a narcotics addict, a robber and a killer—they still love him. They would do anything to help him, and restore him.

Can you see the parallels between God and those parents? God doesn't want us to suffer. He does everything he can to keep us from suffering, or inflicting suffering upon others. He tells us what is right and what is wrong, in order that suffering may be eliminated or kept to a minimum. Yet the freedom he gave us can be used for good or for evil. And as history and experience sadly confirm, that freedom has been abused. Yet God still loves humanity, and is prepared to do anything he can to help them, and restore them to the way he wished. The death of Christ on the cross underscores this point. The pain and suffering of Christ on the cross show us the suffering and pain which human sin are causing God, and invite us to return to him and his ways.

3. Pain and suffering gently bring home to us the fact that we are mortal, and must die. In the last chapter, we noted how humans cannot really bear the thought of death. It is something which they would much prefer to ignore. Suffering and pain are part of a larger picture — the fact that we are mortal and frail humans, who will have to die. We come to see the full importance of the suffering and resurrection of Jesus. As St. Paul emphasizes, resurrection comes through death and suffering: it is by sharing Christ's sufferings and death that we will share in his glorious resurrection (Romans 8:15–18).

4. God knows what it is like to suffer. As we saw in an earlier chapter, the doctrine of the incarnation brings home to us that God knows at first hand what it is like to suffer pain. God doesn't stand aloof from our suffering, but has been through it himself. He knows what it is like. The playlet *The Long Silence* (see p. 37) should be

read again here. We can turn to God in prayer about suffering, knowing that he understands what it is like.

5. Suffering is a mystery, which we shall never fully understand. Martin Luther compares the life of faith to walking in the dark, not being fully able to see the landscape around us. Many things seem strange and unrelated, simply because we cannot see them properly. When the sun rises, of course, we are enabled to see things clearly, and realize the way they relate to each other. Suffering is like something we encounter while walking in the dark. We feel that it ought not to be there, and cannot understand how it came to be there. But we cannot see the whole picture. In the end, Christians believe that they will one day understand the mystery of suffering. One day, its place and purpose in God's loving plan of salvation will become clear. But on that day, we shall be with the Lord, when suffering itself will have passed away (Revelation 21:1–4).

Objection: The idea of a personal God is ridiculous

Some of your friends may argue that the idea of a "personal God" is ridiculous. It's far too unsophisticated for them! When you talk about a "personal" God, they probably conjure up a mental image of an old man with a long beard dressed up in white, sitting on a cloud somewhere unspecified. "How can you expect us to believe in a God like that?" they ask. "It's far too simple!"

An obvious reply is that Christians just *don't* think about God in this way! Newspaper cartoonists certainly do—but the truth of Christianity doesn't depend upon what newspaper cartoonists think God is like! Thinking about God as a person certainly doesn't mean thinking about God as an old man on a cloud. So the first point you could make in response is to criticize this lousy way of thinking about God. However, let's make some more sophisticated points in addition.

1. The idea of an old man up in the sky would just be one way (and not a very good way, and not a particularly *Christian* way!) of visualizing God. In other words, we need some sort of mental picture to help us think about God. But this mental picture isn't the same as the *reality* of God! I could draw a fairly lousy picture of the President of the United States. You might look at the picture and tell me that it's a lousy picture of the President of the United States—and you'd be right! But what you couldn't argue is that the President of the United States didn't exist, just because I had drawn a bad picture of him.

Nor could you conclude that my picture wasn't a representation of the president—it was just a representation that wasn't good enough to do full justice to him. Now the Christian will argue that no representation of God can ever do justice to him. We need simple representations, or mental pictures, of God if we're going to think about him. Christians, of course, would much prefer to use illustrations taken from Scripture— for example, God as a king, as a father, or as a shepherd (rather than an old man on a cloud). Let's look at the mental picture of God as a shepherd (to use a more scriptural way of thinking about God than an old man on a cloud). We might say that God is *like* a shepherd. But this doesn't mean that God *is* a shepherd! Let's take this point a little further.

2. In the natural sciences, models are used to help visualize complex systems. For example, the "kinetic theory of gases" suggests that we think about gas

102

molecules as if they were billiard balls bumping into each other. If we do this, we discover that we can predict some of the properties of gases—for example, the pressure increases when the volume decreases. Now nobody is saying that gas molecules *are* billiard balls! For a start they're much smaller. We're just saying that, in some respects, they *are like* billiard balls. Billiard balls are a useful mental picture of gas molecules, and help us understand the way they behave. In short: they are models of gas molecules.

Now when we talk about God as a person, we aren't saying that God is a human being! What we are saying is that human personal relationships help us understand the way in which God behaves. To put this more formally: human relationships model God. Have you noticed how often Scripture uses human relationships to talk about God? Think of the Parable of the Prodigal Son. Think of how often Scripture talks about God loving us (John 3:16). Think of how often Scripture talks about God forgiving us, or our need to be reconciled to him. These ideas are drawn from human personal relationships. Just as billiard balls help us visualize and understand gas molecules, so these human personal relationships help us visualize and understand God.

So when we talk about God as a person, we are affirming a whole series of central biblical insights. We aren't saying that God is another human being. We are saying that Christians understand God to behave in ways which are paralleled in the best human relationships. It means discarding inadequate ideas about God—like God as an abstract idea—and affirming the biblical witness to God as one who loves us, meets us, and enters into a relationship with us. Prayer, after all, is basically like talking to another person (notice how Jesus makes this point: Matthew 7:9–11). Christians have to do justice to the way in which God reveals himself in Scripture, and the way in which Christians have experienced him down the ages. And the idea of a "personal God" and of our relation with him as a "personal relationship" is a very helpful and proper way of talking and thinking about the "God and Father of our Lord Jesus Christ" (1 Peter 1:3).

Much the same thing can be said about the doctrine of the Trinity, to which we now turn.

Objection: The doctrine of the Trinity is absurd

Many people find the idea of God as "three-in-one" ridiculous. It's just bad celestial mathematics! And many Christians share the same suspicion—that the doctrine of the Trinity is really just an embarrassment which is best not talked about! For some, it even seems to suggest that there are actually three gods! Yet there is no need to have the slightest anxiety about this doctrine. It expresses some incredibly important insights about God. We're going to look at four ways of making sense of the doctrine, which you will almost certainly find helpful in explaining the doctrine to your puzzled friends.

1. The Trinity tells us what God we're actually talking about

Let's suppose that you are trying to identify a famous public figure. You might go about describing him like this. He escaped from a prisoner of war camp during the Boer War, then he became Lord of the Admiralty during the First World War, and then he became Prime Minister during the Second World War. The person you're describing here, of course, is Winston Churchill. You can think of other people whom you would describe in the same way—you hit the high points of their careers. You give a biographical sketch, if you like.

The doctrine of the Trinity identifies God by hitting the high points of his dealings with us. He is the God who created us and the universe; he is the God who was present in Jesus Christ, and raised him from the dead; he is the God who is still active in his church through the Holy Spirit. Notice how often the New Testament refers to God in this way. For example, Paul talks about God as he "who raised Jesus our Lord from the dead" (Romans 4:24). The doctrine of the Trinity answers the questions: "What God are you actually talking about?" We are talking about the God who created us, who redeemed us through Jesus Christ, and who is now present with us through his Spirit.

2. The Trinity identifies three essential features of the understanding of God

The Christian understanding of God is incredibly rich and deep, and very difficult to put into words. Words may well fail us as we try to do justice to the full breadth of our experience of the loving and living God. So where do you start? The doctrine of the Trinity sketches the basic outline of the Christian doctrine of God. The details you can fill in later. Let's give an illustration to see how this works.

A very helpful way of understanding the full significance of Jesus Christ is sometimes referred to as "the three-fold office of Christ." The Old Testament seems to define three "offices" or "roles" which are of major importance: the prophet, who declares the will of God to his people; the king, who rules over his people; and the priest, who makes sacrifices for the sins of his people. The Old Testament points ahead to the future fulfillment of these roles—for example, it talks about the coming of a prophet who, like Moses, would see God face to face (Deuteronomy 34:10). It talks about the coming of a future king, a descendant of David, who would rule over a redeemed Israel (2 Samuel 7:12–16). And the New Testament sees these three roles as being brought together in Jesus.

Jesus is a prophet (Matthew 21:11; Luke 7:16), a priest (Hebrews 2:17; 3:1) and a king (Matthew 21:5; 27:11). He declares God's will to his people, he rules over them, and he gave himself as a sacrifice for their sin. Now nobody is saying that there are three Jesus Christs! What we are saying is that this one person, Jesus Christ, brings together in himself three great Old Testament roles. In order to do justice to the biblical understanding of who Jesus is and why he matters, we have to include all these three roles. They are the basic building-blocks of our understanding of Jesus. To leave out one or two of them results in a seriously inadequate view of Jesus.

Now this is a very helpful way of beginning to think about the significance of Jesus and explaining it to your friends. But it is also very helpful in beginning to think about the Trinity. The doctrine of the Trinity tells us that there are three different central roles played by God himself. He is the creator of the world. He is the redeemer of the world, through the death and resurrection of Jesus Christ. And he is the sanctifier, through the work of the Holy Spirit. All these are the work of the one and the same God. Yet they are not the same: each is distinct. To leave out any one of them leads to an inadequate view of God. You might like to think of a play, in which there are three great central roles. The doctrine of the Trinity tells us that the three great roles in the drama of human redemption are all played by God himself. To put it another way, the doctrine of the Trinity spells out the basic elements in the Christian understanding of God.

3. The Trinity as a way of preserving the mystery of God

As we have emphasized, it is impossible to describe God adequately. Human words are just not capable of doing justice to him. The Austrian philosopher Ludwig Wittgenstein remarked that human words weren't capable of describing adequately something as commonplace as the aroma of coffee—and how much less are they capable of describing God! The doctrine of the Trinity is a reminder of the mystery of God—that our experience of God and his revelation of himself to us in Scripture are far too complex to be summed up in a neat formula. The doctrine of the Trinity brings together the central themes of the Christian understanding of God. It doesn't help us to understand God—but it does help us understand how astonishingly rich and profound our experience of him really is.

4. The Trinity as a means of emphasizing God's unity in his actions

Most people normally think of Dorothy L. Sayers as the writer of crime fiction and creator of the famous literary detective Lord Peter Wimsey. However, she was also passionately concerned with explaining and communicating Christian ideas. In her book *The Mind of the Maker,* she develops a very helpful way of thinking about the Trinity. Consider a book, she suggests—for example, Karl Marx's *Das Kapital*. First, this book takes shape in the mind of its writer. Nobody else knows about the book—it's just there in that mind. Then the book is written. The book expresses the thoughts that are already there, but in a way in which others can find out about them. The thoughts that were once just in Marx's mind are now made concrete or objective in the printed volume which results. Third, the book has an impact upon people. They read it and are affected by what they read. Its ideas are acted upon and put into practice. All these are essential aspects of the book. Nobody is saying that there are three *Das Kapitals*—just that there are three aspects of the one book.

Now can you see how this helps us understand what the Trinity is saying? Sayers is arguing that we can distinguish three aspects of a concept: the abstract idea itself, the idea as it is made known through a book, and the idea as it affects people and is put into practice. Yet we aren't dealing with three different ideas—just the same idea, as it is experienced in three different ways.

Now let's consider God and his great plan of redemption for humanity. We can distinguish the same three aspects: God the Father conceives the great plan of salvation, which is made incarnate in Jesus Christ. In Jesus Christ, we see God's plan of salvation published, openly declared. And the Holy Spirit begins the actualization of this plan in the lives of men and women. Throughout the whole drama, it is the same God and the same plan of salvation: it just has different aspects. And so the Trinity emphasizes the unity of God in his plan of salvation for the world.

This analogy has one weakness, which it is important to notice. Every analogy (however useful!) breaks down at points. The doctrine of the Trinity isn't saying that God acts in one way (as Father) before the birth of Jesus, in another (as Son) during the lifetime of Jesus, and in a third (as Holy Spirit) after Pentecost. The doctrine of the Trinity affirms that God acts *throughout history* as Father, Son and Holy Spirit. Even at creation, for example, the three persons may be seen at work. Genesis 1:1–2 brings Father, Word and Spirit together in the great act of creation.

Let's summarize our discussion about the Trinity. Christians have always had a choice when they talk about God. They can talk about him in a really simple way, which everyone can understand—and fail to do justice to the richness of the biblical revelation of God. Or they can try to do justice to that revelation, and end up with a view of God which is difficult to understand. Christians have always felt it right to do justice to God as he has revealed himself, rather than go in for some simple view of God which ignores that revelation. And in the end, the doctrine of the Trinity is a safeguard of the mystery of God. It prevents us from adopting simple and naive views of God, which are easy to understand but fail totally to do justice to God's revelation of himself.

This doesn't mean that you need talk about "the Trinity" all the time! You can just talk, in very simple terms, about "God." The important point to remember is that underneath this very simple view of God is a far from simple reality! It's like the tip of an iceberg: about 90% of its volume lies hidden beneath the surface of the sea. The doctrine of the Trinity is like that part of the iceberg which lies hidden beneath the waves. It's there—but you don't see it. You concern yourself with the bit you can see—its tip. But the doctrine of the Trinity reminds us of how great and wonderful God is, and how inadequate that little three-letter word "God" is to do justice to him.

Questions for discussion

■ What is left of the Marxist critique of Christianity?

■ Does the existence of suffering call the love of God into question?

■ What important insights are safeguarded by the idea of a "personal God?"

■ How would you explain the doctrine of the Trinity?

For further reading

Hans Küng, **Does God Exist?**, pp. 189–339. A very fine presentation and critique of various forms of atheism, including Marxism, which will enable you to deal fully with their arguments against the existence of God. Some may find this demanding reading.

C. S. Lewis, **The Problem of Pain.** Probably the best work written on this problem. Very thoughtful and helpful, with all the clarity and force you'd expect from a writer of this calibre. Worth recommending—or giving!—to a friend who has difficulty in this area.

C. S. Lewis, **"The Weight of Glory."** A famous sermon, in which Lewis develops his "argument from desire" for the existence of God. A particularly helpful piece of writing for those studying literature.

Alister E. McGrath, **Understanding the Trinity.** An easy-to-read study of the arguments for and against God's existence, the idea of a personal God, and the doctrine of the Trinity. It develops the ideas noted in the present chapter.

J. I. Packer, **Knowing God.** A very helpful study of many aspects of the scriptural understanding of God.

For Further Reading

Craig Blomberg, **The Historical Reliability of the Gospels** (InterVarsity).

David Cook, **Thinking about Faith** (Zondervan).

R. T. France, **The Evidence for Jesus** (InterVarsity).

Michael Green, **The Day Death Died** (InterVarsity).

———, **The Empty Cross of Jesus** (InterVarsity).

———, **World on the Run** (Servant Press).

———, **You must be Joking!** (Hodder & Stoughton).

Hans Küng, **Does God Exist?** (Random House).

C. S. Lewis, **Mere Christianity** (Macmillan).

———, **The Problem of Pain** (Macmillan).

———, **Surprised by Joy** (Harcourt Brace Jovanovich).

———, **"The Weight of Glory,"** in *Screwtape Proposes a Toast* (Macmillan), pp. 94–111.

Alister E. McGrath, **Understanding Jesus** (Zondervan).

———, **Understanding the Trinity** (Zondervan).

I. H. Marshall, **The Work of Christ** (Paternoster Press).

Stephen Neill, **The Supremacy of Jesus** (InterVarsity).

J. I. Packer, **Evangelism and the Sovereignty of God** (InterVarsity).

———, **Knowing God** (InterVarsity).

Francis Schaeffer, **The God Who is There** (InterVarsity).

John Stott, **Basic Christianity** (Eerdmans).

———, **The Cross of Christ** (InterVarsity).